THE

1863

LAWS OF WAR

THE
1863
LAWS OF WAR

BEING THE

I.

ARTICLES OF WAR

AN ACT FOR ESTABLISHING RULES AND ARTICLES FOR THE
GOVERNMENT OF THE ARMIES OF THE UNITED STATES

April 10, 1806

(As Amended through June 1863)

II.

GENERAL ORDERS 100

INSTRUCTIONS FOR THE GOVERNMENT OF THE ARMIES
OF THE UNITED STATES IN THE FIELD

April 24, 1863

III.

GENERAL ORDERS 49

ORDER FOR THE MAKING AND GRANTING OF PAROLES

February 28, 1863

IV.

EXTRACTS OF REVISED ARMY REGULATIONS OF 1861

WITH AN APPENDIX CONTAINING CHANGES AND LAWS AFFECTING
ARMY REGULATIONS TO JUNE 25, 1863

STACKPOLE
BOOKS

STACKPOLE BOOKS
5067 Ritter Road
Mechanicsburg, PA 17055
www.stackpolebooks.com

Printed in the United States of America

10 9 8 7 6 5 4 3 2 1

Library of Congress Cataloging-in-Publication Data

The 1863 laws of war / War Department.
     p. cm.
  Includes bibliographical references.
  ISBN-13: 978-0-8117-0133-4 (alk. paper)
  1. United States—History—Civil War, 1861–1865—Law and legislation.
2. War and emergency legislation—United States—History. 3. Military
law—United States—History.
  KF7221.A1863 2005
  343.73'01—dc22

                                                2005007827

ISBN 0-8117-0133-6

TABLE OF CONTENTS

PART I:

ARTICLES OF WAR

**An Act for Establishing Rules and Articles
for the Government of the Armies of the United States,
April 10, 1806, As Amended through June 25, 1863**

PART II:

GENERAL ORDERS 100

Instructions for the Government of the Armies of the United States in the Field, April 24, 1863

PART III:

GENERAL ORDERS 49

Order for the Making and Granting of Paroles, February 28, 1863

PART IV:

Extracts of Revised United States Army Regulations of 1861 with an Appendix containing the Changes and Laws Affecting Army Regulations to June 25, 1863

INTRODUCTION

FROM its inception as a nation, America has venerated the rule of law. The armed forces of the United States have, at least since 1806, had laws governing the activity of the army and navy both in times of peace and when at war. The laws governing the military forces were, for the most part, passed as acts of Congress. Some were in themselves specific laws, such as the *Articles of War*. Other laws were contained in army regulations, presidential directives, and authorities granted under other laws allowing commanders of the army to promulgate decrees called "general orders." Violations of the *Articles of War*, general orders, and army regulations were punishable by court-martial.

The advent of the American Civil War (1861–1865) resulted in a considerable expansion in the laws governing the conduct of warfare, especially General Order No. 100, or the "Lieber Code" as it was commonly called. The effect of this originally American code was so profound that the code was adopted into the laws and customs of war of several nations and included later into the Hague and Geneva Conventions.

Four such laws of war are contained in this book. Together, they offer considerable insight into how the army was governed, controlled, and operated. These laws are a valuable historical reference into the times of the Civil War, and they are also instructive and fascinating reading, sort of a commentary of man's attempts to control the ravages of warfare. That they were strictly adhered to by both the Union and Confederate armies is a testament to relatively homogeneous nature of American society in the mid-nineteenth century.

I. Articles of War: An Act for Establishing Rules and Articles for the Government of the Armies of the United States, April 10, 1806 (as amended through June 25, 1863).

The first set of laws is the *Articles of War*, properly titled: *An Act for Establishing Rules and Articles for the Government of the Armies of the United States*. The joint act of Congress establishing the *Articles of War* was first passed on April 10, 1806. The *Articles* were modified once by the act of May 29, 1830. In 1861, they were again revised. Further amendments up to June 25, 1863 are included in the articles as noted.

The *Articles of War* are the predecessor of the modern-day *Uniform Code of Military Justice*. The *Articles* governed the discipline and behavior of soldiers toward superiors, toward each other, toward the enemy, and for performance of their sworn duties as soldiers. The *Articles* were the basis for discipline in the ranks. Violations of the *Articles* were punishable by the military authorities. Adjudication of violators was by regimental and/or general courts-martial, procedures for which are also contained in the *Articles* and in the *Revised Army Regulations*. Punishments ranged from death and imprisonment, to dismissal from the service, forfeitures of pay, and reprimand. For example, the second article of war states that officers behaving indecently or irreverently in any place of worship are to be brought before a court-martial and "severely" reprimanded. Non-commissioned officers caught uttering a "profane oath" were fined one dollar for the first offense. Proceeds from such fines were to go to the regimental or company fund for the benefit of sick soldiers. Sending a challenge to a duel risked being cashiered from the service. More serious offenses such as desertion in time of war, divulging a password to the enemy, and like matters were punishable by death or as directed by court-martial.

As of June 25, 1863, there were 102 Articles of War, one of which had not yet been numbered.

II. General Orders 100: Instructions for the Government of the Armies of the United States *in the Field*, April 24, 1863.

One of the most profound sets of laws to emerge from the American Civil War was General Orders No. 100, *Instructions for the Government of Armies of the United States in the Field*, written at the direction of President Lincoln by Professor Francis Lieber, and promulgated on April 24, 1863.

By 1862, Lincoln was concerned about the inhumanity of war between two sets of Americans, threats of retaliation against prisoners of war on both sides, and about the effects of war on noncombatant civilians. Lincoln was a healer; he wished to avoid development of civil hatred that might not heal when the war ended. To achieve this, he directed Professor Lieber, through General-in-Chief Henry W. Halleck, to write a code of wartime conduct for Union forces on the battlefield.

Lieber, a doctor of philosophy and law, was born in Germany. He fought with Blücher at Waterloo in 1815 and in Greece's 1820 war of independence. He taught at the University of Jena in Germany and immigrated to the United States in 1827. He taught international law at South Carolina College and Columbia University in New York.

In 1862, his writings and lectures on aspects of the law and usage of war caught the attention of General Halleck, who was searching for guidance to give the army regarding treatment of guerrilla forces then harassing the Union army. Lieber, however, had a broader concept in mind, namely a definitive work on the laws and usage of war, and with President Lincoln's support, the project commenced.

Military leaders from antiquity on set down rules and regulations to discipline their troops. The Romans had detailed rules, and so did the United States after the act of 1806, the date of the original *Articles of War* cited above. But these rules, for the most part, were designed for the internal discipline of the army. Few rules existed for treatment of the enemy or civilian populations, or unconventional forces (partisans and guerrillas) that emerged in the course of the American Civil War.

Theories on the laws of war between nations in the Christian tradition have a long history. Church leaders first attempted to bring notions of morality and humane treatment into war. Among the earliest attempts are the fifth-century writings of St. Augustine, bishop of Hippo. In his *City of God*, Augustine proceeds to define a "just war" and some of the permitted and proscribed acts of armies vis-à-vis each other and the innocent civilian population. Through the centuries, law-of-war theorists in Europe developed certain touchstones of what was moral and immoral in war, which they purported to be universally binding in the relations between nations. Later writers, such as Machiavelli and Clausewitz, added their thoughts on the nature of war. Yet, there was no one synthesized, comprehensive law of land warfare that laid down in clear, explicit, formal terms the rights and obligations of one's own army and those of an enemy's army and the civilian population until that produced by Francis Lieber in 1863.

The Lieber Code contains ten themes. These were important themes that addressed problems directly associated with the circumstances being experienced by the Union and Confederate armies. As a "general order," it had to be obeyed by Union Forces. Upon learning of its enactment, the Confederate commissioner inquired if the order was really going to be enforced within the Union army, or whether it was meant to apply only to Confederate forces. The answer was "yes"; it would be enforced in the Union army.

General Orders 100 had a profound effect on the international law of land warfare. The governments of Great Britain, France, and Prussia copied it. The Geneva Conventions of 1864/1868 and the Hague Convention of 1907 adopted Lieber's Code, and these conventions were ratified by nearly all the civilized countries for implementation by their armies in the field.

III. General Orders No. 49: Order for the Making and Granting of Paroles, February 28, 1863

Rather than process thousands of prisoners of war in battle, many Union commanders began to issue paroles, whereby a captured Confederate soldier would be released from custody on his promise not to engage in fighting until he was duly exchanged for a Union prisoner of war. It was a loose system, and many so-called parolees simply joined a new unit and continued to fight.

To bring order to the system, Gen. Henry W. Halleck, General-in-Chief of the Union armies, issued General Orders No. 49 stipulating ground rules for making and giving paroles. Records were to be kept and prisoners handled in accordance with the new procedures. There were to be no more battlefield paroles. The choices were two: become a prisoner of war and await exchange of prisoners (negotiated by Union and Confederate agents for the exchange of prisoners) in a prisoner of war compound, or make a formal, recorded parole promise not to engage in armed conflict until exchanged. Giving a prisoner the latter option now required strict approval of higher authorities, with approval depending largely on the rank of the prisoner.

By the date of this general order, the Union army had a commissary-general for prisoners to oversee Union prisoner of war camps, and both the Union and Confederate armies had agents who negotiated the exchange of prisoners in accordance with this general order.

IV. Extracts of Revised United States Army Regulations of 1861, with an Appendix Containing Changes Affecting Army Regulations to June 25, 1863.

By mid-1863, the mobilization of the army, experience in the field, and technical developments resulted in so many changes to the *Revised Regulations* of 1861 that publication of a separate book to catalog them was required. The book was the *Revised*

United States Army Regulations of 1861, with an Appendix Containing the Changes and Laws Affecting Army Regulations and Articles of War to June 25, 1863.

Army regulations in the Civil War consisted of 52 articles encompassing 1,676 paragraphs that provided "how-to" information regarding the administrative and tactical operations of the Army. The appendix contains 136 changes to the regulations that were introduced between the years 1861 and June 25, 1863. These changes revised or added to the general regulations of the army as well as to the regulations and instructions governing the various staff departments (Quartermaster, Recruiting Service, Ordnance Department, Pay Department, Commissary, etc.). In addition, there were six pages of extracts from acts of Congress giving the army guidance on various topics, primarily on the organization and pay of the army.

Army regulations were written by the army and were intended to contain all of the rules and instructions for operating the day-to-day army in the field and in garrison. But, the expansion of the army and the introduction of new equipment and weapons soon generated the need for much highly detailed technical information, such as forms and formats for correspondence, records formats, and similar minutia that later would be put into field manuals. In fact, by 1863, several sections of the *Regulations*, such as those dealing with engineer operations and technical ordnance specifications, had already been converted to separate manuals.

The extracts from the army regulations contained in this book are based primarily on Brig. Gen. Daniel Butterfield's extracts of Army *Regulations* "that should be known by every soldier," plus many additional ones selected by the publisher. Our selection portrays the important aspects of military operations addressed in each of the 52 articles.

PART I.

Articles of War:
An Act for Establishing Rules and
Articles for the Government of
the Armies of the United States,
April 10, 1806, as Amended
through June 25, 1863

ARTICLES OF WAR.

AN ACT FOR ESTABLISHING RULES AND ARTICLES FOR THE GOVERNMENT OF THE ARMIES OF THE UNITED STATES.*

SECTION I. *Be it enacted, by the Senate and House of Representatives of the United States of America, in Congress assembled,* That, from and after the passing of this act, the following shall be the rules and articles by which the armies of the United States shall be governed:

ARTICLE 1. Every officer now in the army of the United States shall, in six months from the passing of this act, and every officer who shall hereafter be appointed shall, before he enters on the duties of his office, subscribe these rules and regulations.

ART. 2. It is earnestly recommended to all officers and soldiers diligently to attend divine service; and all officers who shall behave indecently or irreverently at any place of divine worship shall, if commissioned officers, be brought before a general court-martial, there to be publicly and severely reprimanded by the president; if non-commissioned officers or soldiers, every person so offending shall, for his first offense, forfeit one-sixth of a dollar, to be deducted out of his next pay; for the second offense, he shall not only forfeit a like sum, but be confined twenty-four hours; and for every like offense, shall suffer and pay in like

---

*These rules and articles, with the exceptions indicated by the notes annexed to articles 10, 20, 55, 65, and 87, remain unaltered, and in force at present [July 25, 1863].

3

manner; which money, so forfeited, shall be applied, by the captain or senior officer of the troop or company, to the use of the sick soldiers of the company or troop to which the offender belongs.

ART. 3.   Any non-commissioned officer or soldier who shall use any profane oath or execration, shall incur the penalties expressed in the foregoing article; and a commissioned officer shall forfeit and pay, for each and every such offense, one dollar, to be applied as in the preceding article.

ART. 4.   Every chaplain commissioned in the army or armies of the United States, who shall absent himself from the duties assigned him (excepting in cases of sickness or leave of absence), shall, on conviction thereof before a court-martial, be fined not exceeding one month's pay, besides the loss of his pay during his absence; or be discharged, as the said court-martial shall judge proper.

ART. 5.   Any officer or soldier who shall use contemptuous or disrespectful words against the President of the United States, against the Vice-President thereof, against the Congress of the United States, or against the Chief Magistrate or Legislature of any of the United States in which he may be quartered, if a commissioned officer, shall be cashiered, or otherwise punished, as a court-martial shall direct; if a non-commissioned officer or soldier, he shall suffer such punishment as shall be inflicted upon him by the sentence of a court-martial.

ART. 6.   Any officer or soldier who shall behave himself with contempt or disrespect toward his commanding officer, shall be punished, according to the nature of his offense, by the judgment of a court-martial.

ART. 7.   Any officer or soldier who shall begin, excite, cause, or join in, any mutiny or sedition, in any troop or company in the service of the United States, or in any party, post, detachment, or guard, shall suffer death, or such other punishment as by a court-martial shall be inflicted.

ART. 8.   Any officer, non-commissioned officer, or soldier, who, being present at any mutiny or sedition, does not use his utmost endeavor to suppress the same, or, coming to the knowledge of any intended mutiny, does not, without delay, give information thereof to his commanding officer, shall be punished by the sentence of a court-martial with death, or otherwise, according to the nature of his offense.

ART. 9.   Any officer or soldier who shall strike his superior officer, or draw or lift up any weapon, or offer any violence against him, being in the execution of his office, on any pretense whatsoever, or shall disobey any lawful command of his superior officer, shall suffer death, or such other punishment as shall, according to the nature of his offense, be inflicted upon him by the sentence of a court-martial.

ART. 10.   Every non-commissioned officer or soldier, who shall enlist himself in the service of the United States, shall, at the time of his so enlisting, or within six days afterward, have the Articles for the government of the armies of the United States read to him, and shall, by the officer who enlisted him, or by the commanding officer of the troop or company into which he was enlisted, be taken before the next justice of the peace, or chief magistrate of any city or town corporate, not being an officer of the army, or, where recourse cannot be had to the civil magistrate, before the judge advocate*, and in his presence shall take the following oath or affirmation:

"I, A. B., do solemnly swear, or affirm (as the case may be), that I will bear true allegiance to the United States of America, and that I will serve them honestly and faithfully

---

*By Sect. 11 of Chap. 42 August 3, 1861, the oath of enlistment and re-enlistment may be administered by any commissioned officer of the army.

against all their enemies or opposers whatsoever; and observe and obey the orders of the President of the United States, and the orders of the officers appointed over me, according to the Rules and Articles for the government of the armies of the United States."

Which justice, magistrate, or judge advocate is to give to the officer a certificate, signifying that the man enlisted did take the said oath or affirmation.

ART. 11. After a non-commissioned officer or soldier shall have been duly enlisted and sworn, he shall not be dismissed from the service without a discharge in writing; and no discharge granted to him shall be sufficient which is not signed by a field officer of the regiment to which he belongs, or commanding officer, where no field officer of the regiment is present; and no discharge shall be given to a non-commissioned officer or soldier before his term of service has expired, but by order of the President, the Secretary of War, the commanding officer of a department, or the sentence of a general court-martial; nor shall a commissioned officer be discharged from the service but by the order of the President of the United States, or by sentence of a general court-martial.

ART. 12. Every colonel, or other officer commanding a regiment, troop or company, and actually quartered with it, may give furloughs to non-commissioned officers or soldiers, in such numbers, and for so long a time, as he shall judge to be most consistent with the good of the service; and a captain, or other inferior officer, commanding a troop or company, or in any garrison, fort, or barrack of the United States (his field officer being absent), may give furloughs to non-commissioned officers or soldiers, for a time not exceeding twenty days in six months, but not to more than two persons to be absent at the same time, excepting some extraordinary occasion should, require it.

ART. 13.   At every muster, the commanding officer of each regiment, troop, or company, there present, shall give to the commissary of musters, or other officer who musters the said regiment, troop, or company, certificates signed by himself, signifying how long such officers, as shall not appear at the said muster, have been absent, and the reason of their absence. In like manner, the commanding officer of every troop or company shall give certificates, signifying the reasons of the absence of the non-commissioned officers and private soldiers; which reasons and time of absence shall be inserted in the muster-rolls, opposite the names of the respective absent officers and soldiers. The certificate shall, together with the muster-rolls, be remitted by the commissary of musters, or other officer mustering, to the Department of War, as speedily as the distance of the place will admit.

ART. 14.   Every officer who shall be convicted before a general court-martial of having signed a false certificate relating to the absence of either officer or private soldier, or relative to his or their pay, shall be cashiered.

ART. 15.   Every officer who shall knowingly make a false muster of man or horse, and every officer or commissary of musters who shall willingly sign, direct, or allow the signing of muster-rolls wherein such false muster is contained, shall, upon proof made thereof, by two witnesses, before a general court-martial, be cashiered, and shall be thereby utterly disabled to have or hold any office or employment in the service of the United States.

ART. 16.   Any commissary of musters, or other officer, who shall be convicted of having taken money, or other thing, by way of gratification, on mustering any regiment, troop, or company, or on signing muster-rolls, shall be displaced from his office, and shall be thereby utterly disabled to have or hold any office or employment in the service of the United States.

ART. 17. Any officer who shall presume to muster a person as a soldier who is not a soldier, shall be deemed guilty of having made a false muster, and shall suffer accordingly.

ART. 18. Every officer who shall knowingly make a false return to the Department of War, or to any of his superior officers, authorized to call for such returns, of the state of the regiment, troop, or company, or garrison, under his command; or of the arms, ammunition, clothing, or other stores thereunto belonging, shall, on conviction thereof before a court-martial, be cashiered.

ART. 19. The commanding officer of every regiment, troop, or independent company, or garrison of the United States, shall, in the beginning of every month, remit, through the proper channels, to the Department of War, an exact return of the regiment, troop, independent company, or garrison, under his command, specifying the names of the officers then absent from their posts, with the reasons for and the time of their absence. And any officer who shall be convicted of having, through neglect or design, omitted sending such returns, shall be punished, according to the nature of his crime, by the judgment of a general court-martial.

ART. 20. All officers and soldiers who have received pay, or have been duly enlisted in the service of the United States, and shall be convicted of having deserted the same, shall suffer death, or such other punishment as, by sentence of a court-martial, shall be inflicted.*

ART. 21. Any non-commissioned officer or soldier who shall, without leave from his commanding officer, absent himself from his troop, company, or detachment, shall, upon being convicted thereof, be punished according to the nature of his offense, at the discretion of a court-martial.

---

*No officer or soldier in the army of the United States shall be subject to the punishment of death, for desertion in time of peace.—*Act*-29*th May*, 1830.

ART. 22.   No non-commissioned officer or soldier shall enlist himself in any other regiment, troop, or company, without a regular discharge from the regiment, troop, or company in which he last served, on the penalty of being reputed a deserter and suffering accordingly. And in case any officer shall knowingly receive and entertain such non-commissioned officer or soldier, or shall not, after his being discovered to be a deserter, immediately confine him, and give notice thereof to the corps in which he last served, the said officer shall, by a court-martial, be cashiered.

ART. 23.   Any officer or soldier who shall be convicted of having advised or persuaded any other officer or soldier to desert the service of the United States, shall suffer death, or such other punishment as shall be inflicted upon him by the sentence of a court-martial.

ART. 24.   No officer or soldier shall use any reproachful or provoking speeches or gestures to another, upon pain, if an officer, of being put in arrest; if a soldier, confined, and of asking pardon of the party offended, in the presence of his commanding officer.

ART. 25.   No officer or soldier shall send a challenge to another officer or soldier, to fight a duel, or accept a challenge if sent, upon pain, if a commissioned officer, of being cashiered; if a non-commissioned officer or soldier, of suffering corporeal punishment, at the discretion of a court-martial.

ART. 26.   If any commissioned or non-commissioned officer commanding a guard shall knowingly or willingly suffer any person whatsoever to go forth to fight a duel, he shall be punished as a challenger; and all seconds, promoters, and carriers of challenges, in order to duels, shall be deemed principals, and be punished accordingly. And it shall be the duty of every officer commanding an army, regiment, company, post, or detachment, who is knowing of a challenge being given or accepted by any officer, non-commissioned officer, or soldier under his command, or has reason to believe the same to be the case, immediately to arrest and bring to trial such offenders.

ART. 27.   All officers, of what condition soever, have power to part and quell all quarrels, frays, and disorders, though the persons concerned should belong to another regiment, troop, or company; and either to order officers into arrest, or non-commissioned officers or soldiers into confinement, until their proper superior officers shall be acquainted therewith; and whosoever shall refuse to obey such officers (though of an inferior rank), or shall draw his sword upon him, shall be punished at the discretion of a general court-martial.

ART. 28.   Any officer or soldier who shall upbraid another for refusing a challenge, shall himself be punished as a challenger; and all officers and soldiers are hereby discharged for any disgrace or opinion of disadvantage which might arise from their having refused to accept of challenges, as they will only have acted in obedience to the laws, and done their duty as good soldiers who subject themselves to discipline.

ART. 29.   No sutler shall be permitted to sell any kind of liquors or victuals, or to keep their houses or shops open for the entertainment of soldiers, after nine at night, or before the beating of the reveille, or upon Sundays, during divine service or sermon, on the penalty of being dismissed from all future sutling.

ART. 30.   All officers commanding in the field, forts, barracks, or garrisons of the United States, are hereby required to see that the persons admitted to suttle shall supply the soldiers with good and wholesome provisions, or other articles, at a reasonable price, as they shall be answerable for their neglect.

ART. 31.   No officer commanding in any of the garrisons, forts, or barracks of the United States, shall exact exorbitant prices for houses or stalls let out to sutlers, or connive at the like exactions of others; nor by his own authority, and for his private advantage, lay any duty or imposition upon, or be interested in, the sale of any victuals, liquors, or other necessaries of life brought into the garrison, fort, or barracks, for the use of the soldiers, on the penalty of being discharged from the service.

ART. 32. Every officer commanding in quarters, garrisons, or on the march, shall keep good order, and, to the utmost of his power, redress all abuses or disorders which may be committed by any officer or soldier under his command; if, upon complaint made to him of officers or soldiers beating or otherwise ill-treating any person, or disturbing fairs or markets, or of committing any kind of riots, to the disquieting of the citizens of the United States, he, the said commander, who shall refuse or omit to see justice done to the offender or offenders, and reputation made to the party or parties injured, as far as part of the offender's pay shall enable him or them, shall, upon proof thereof, be cashiered, or otherwise punished, as a general court-martial shall direct.

ART. 33. When any commissioned officer or soldier shall be accused of a capital crime, or of having used violence, or committed any offense against the person or property of any citizen of any of the United States, such as it is punishable by the known laws of the land, the commanding officer and officers of every regiment, troop, or company, to which the person or persons so accused shall belong, are hereby required, upon application duly made by, or in behalf of, the party or parties injured, to use their utmost endeavors to deliver over such accused person or persons to the civil magistrate, and likewise to the aiding and assisting to the officers of justice in apprehending and securing the person or persons so accused, in order to bring him or them to trial. If any commanding officer or officers shall willfully neglect, or shall refuse, upon the application aforesaid, to deliver over such accused person or persons to the civil magistrates, or to be aiding and assisting to the officers of justice in apprehending such person or persons, the officer or officers so offending shall be cashiered.

ART. 34. If any officer shall think himself wronged by his Colonel, or the commanding officer of the regiment, and shall, upon due application being made to him, be refused redress, he may complain to the General commanding in the State or Territory where such regiment shall be stationed, in order to obtain justice; who is hereby required to examine into said complaint, and take proper measures for redressing the wrong complained of, and transmit, as soon as possible, to the Department of War, a true state of such complaint, with the proceedings had thereof.

ART. 35. If any inferior officer or soldier shall think himself wronged by his Captain or other officer, he is to complain thereof to the commanding officer of the regiment, who is hereby required to summon a regimental court-martial, for the doing justice to the complaint; from which regimental court-martial either party may, if he thinks himself still aggrieved, appeal to a general court-martial. But if, upon a second hearing, the appeal shall appear vexatious and groundless, the person so appealing shall be punished at the discretion of the said court-martial.

ART. 36. Any commissioned officer, store-keeper, or commissary, who shall be convicted at a general court-martial of having sold, without a proper order for that purpose, embezzled, misapplied, or willfully, or through neglect, suffered any of the provisions, forage, arms, clothing, ammunition, or other military stores belonging to the United States to be spoiled or damaged, shall, at his own expense, make good the loss or damage, and shall, moreover, forfeit all his pay, and be dismissed from the service.

ART. 37. Any non-commissioned officer or soldier who shall be convicted before a regimental court-martial of having sold, or designedly, or through neglect, wasted the ammunition delivered out to him, to be employed in the service of the United States, shall be punished at the discretion of such court.

ART. 38. Every non-commissioned officer or soldier who shall be convicted at a regimental court-martial of having sold, lost, or spoiled, through neglect, his horse, arms, clothes, or accoutrements, shall undergo such weekly stoppage (not exceeding the half of his pay) as such court-martial shall judge sufficient, for repairing the loss or damage; and shall suffer confinement, or such other corporeal punishment as his crime shall deserve.

ART. 39.   Every officer who shall be convicted before a court-martial of having embezzled or misapplied any money with which he may have been entrusted, for the payment of the men under his command, or for enlisting men into the service, or for other purposes, if a commissioned officer, shall be cashiered, and compelled to refund the money; if a non-commissioned officer, shall be reduced to the ranks, be put under stoppages until the money be made good, and suffer such corporeal punishment as such court-martial shall direct.

ART. 40.   Every captain of a troop or company is charged with the arms, accoutrements, ammunition, clothing, or other warlike stores belonging to the troop or company under his command, which he is to be accountable for to his Colonel in case of their being lost, spoiled, or damaged, not by unavoidable accidents, or on actual service.

ART. 41.   All non-commissioned officers and soldiers who shall be found one mile from the camp without leave, in writing, from their commanding officer, shall suffer such punishment as shall be inflicted upon them by the sentence of a court-martial.

ART. 42.   No officer or soldier shall lie out of his quarters, garrison, or camp without leave from his superior officer, upon penalty of being punished, according to the nature of his offense by the sentence of court-martial.

ART. 43.   Every non-commissioned officer and soldier shall retire to his quarters or tent at the beating of the retreat; in default of which he shall be punished according to the nature of his offense.

ART. 44.   No officer, non-commissioned officer, or soldier shall fail in repairing, at the time fixed, to the place of parade, of exercise, or other rendezvous appointed by his commanding officer, if not prevented by sickness or some other evident necessity, or shall go from the said place of rendezvous without leave from his commanding officer, before he shall be regularly dismissed or relieved, on the penalty of being punished, according to the nature of his offense, by the sentence of a court-martial.

ART. 45.   Any commissioned officer who shall be found drunk on his guard, party, or other duty, shall be cashiered. Any non-commissioned officer or soldier so offending shall suffer such corporeal punishment as shall be inflicted by the sentence of a court-martial.

ART. 46.   Any sentinel who shall be found sleeping on his post, or shall leave it before he shall be regularly relieved, shall suffer death, or such other punishment as shall be inflicted by the sentence of a court martial.

ART. 47.   No soldier belonging to any regiment, troop, or company shall hire another to do his duty for him, or be excused from duty but in cases of sickness, disability, or leave of absence; and every such soldier found guilty of hiring his duty, as also the party so hired to do another's duty, shall be punished at the discretion of a regimental court-martial.

ART. 48.   And every non-commissioned officer conniving at such hiring of duty unforesaid, shall be reduced; and every commissioned officer knowing and allowing such ill practices in the service, shall be punished by the judgment of a general court-martial.

ART. 49.   Any officer belonging to the service of the United States, who, by discharging of firearms, drawing of swords, beating of drums, or by any other means whatsoever, shall occasion false alarms in camp, garrison, or quarters, shall suffer death, or such other punishment as shall be ordered by the sentence of a general court-martial.

ART. 50. Any officer or soldier who shall, without urgent necessity, or without the leave of his superior officer, quit his guard, platoon, or division, shall be punished, according to the nature of his offense, by the sentence of a court-martial.

ART. 51. No officer or soldier shall do violence to any person who brings provisions or other necessaries to the camp, garrison, or quarters of the forces of the United States, employed in any parts out of the said States, upon the pain of death, or such other punishment as a court-martial shall direct.

ART. 52. Any officer or soldier who shall misbehave himself before the enemy, run away, or shamefully abandon any fort, post, or guard which he or they may be commanded to defend, or speak words inducing others to do the like, or shall cast away his arms and ammunition, or who shall quit his post or colors to plunder and pillage, every such offender, being duly convicted thereof, shall suffer death, or such other punishment as shall be ordered by the sentence of a general court-martial.

ART. 53. Any person belonging to the armies of the United States who shall make known the watchword to any person who is not entitled to receive it according to the rules and discipline of war, or shall presume to give a parole or watchword different from what he received, shall suffer death, or such other punishment as shall be ordered by the sentence of a general court-martial.

ART. 54. All officers and soldiers are to behave themselves orderly in quarters and on their march; and whoever shall commit any waste or spoil, either in walks of trees, parks, warrens, fish-ponds, houses, or gardens, corn-fields, inclosures of meadows, or shall maliciously destroy any property whatsoever belonging to the inhabitants of the United States, unless by order of the then commander-in-chief of the armies of said States, shall (besides such penalties as they are liable to by law) be punished according to the nature and degree of the offense, by the judgment of a general court-martial.

ART. 55.   Whosoever, belonging to the armies of the United States in foreign parts, shall force a safeguard, shall suffer death.[*]

ART. 56.   Whosoever shall relieve the enemy with money, victuals, or ammunition, or shall knowingly harbor or protect an enemy, shall suffer death, or such other punishment as shall by ordered by the sentence of a court-martial.

ART. 57.   Whosoever shall be convicted of holding correspondence with, or giving intelligence to, the enemy, either directly or indirectly, shall suffer death, or such other punishment as shall be ordered by the sentence of a general court-martial.

ART. 58.   All public stores taken in the enemy's camp, towns, forts, or magazines, whether of artillery, ammunition, clothing, forage or provisions, shall be secured for the service of the United States; for the neglect of which the commanding officer is to be answerable.

ART. 59.   If any commander of the garrison, fortress, or post shall be compelled, by the officers and soldiers under his command, to give up to the enemy, or to abandon it, the commissioned officers, non-commissioned officers, or soldiers who shall be convicted of having so offended, shall suffer death, or such other punishment as shall be inflicted upon them by the sentence of a court-martial.

ART. 60.   All sutlers and retainers to the camp, and all persons whatsoever, serving with the armies of the United States in the field, though not enlisted soldiers, are to be subject to orders, according to the rules and discipline of war.

---

[*]Modified by Sect. 5 Act of Congress [1861]: Whoever, belonging to the armies of the United States in foreign parts, or at any place within the United States or their Territories, during rebellion against the supreme authority of the United States, shall force a safeguard, shall suffer death. *Approved February 13, 1862.*

Art. 61. Officers having brevets or commissions of a prior date to those of the regiment in which they serve, may take place in courts-martial and on detachments, when composed of different corps, according to the ranks given them in their brevets or dates of their former commissions; but in the regiment, troop, or company to which such officers belong, they shall do duty and take rank, both in courts-martial and on detachments which shall be composed of their own corps, according to the commissions by which they are mustered in the said corps.

Art. 62. If, upon marches, guards, or in quarters, different corps of the army shall happen to join, or do duty together, the officer highest in rank of the line of the army, marine corps, or militia, by commission, there on duty or in quarters, shall command the whole, and give orders for what is needful to the service, unless otherwise specially directed by the President of the United States, according to the nature of the case.

Art. 63. The functions of the engineers being generally confined to the most elevated branch of military science, they are not to assume, nor are they subject to be ordered on any duty beyond the line of their immediate profession, except by the special order of the President of the United States; but they are to receive every mark of respect to which their rank in the army may entitle them respectively, and are liable to be transferred, at the discretion of the President, from one corps to another, regard being paid to rank.

Art. 64. General courts-martial may consist of any number of commissioned officers, from five to thirteen, inclusively; but they shall not consist of less than thirteen where that number can be convened without manifest injury to the service.

Art. 65.* Any general officer commanding an army, or Colonel commanding a separate department, may appoint general

---

*[Modified by the Act of 29th May 1830.]—Whenever a general officer commanding an army, or a colonel commanding a separate department, shall be the accuser or prosecutor of any officer in the army of the United States under his command, the general court-martial for the trial of such officer shall be appointed by the President of the United States. continued on page 18

courts-martial whenever necessary. But no sentence of a court-martial shall be carried into execution until after the whole proceedings shall have been laid before the officer ordering the same, or the officer commanding the troops for the time being; neither shall any sentence of a general court-martial, in the time of peace, extending to the loss of life, or the dismission of a commissioned officer, or which shall, either in time of peace or war, respect a general officer, be carried into execution, until after the whole proceedings shall have been transmitted to the Secretary of War, to be laid before the President of the United States for his confirmation or disapproval, and orders in the case. All other sentences may be confirmed and executed by the officer ordering the court to assemble, or the commanding officer for the time being, as the case may be.

ART. 66.   Every officer commanding a regiment or corps may appoint, for his own regiment or corps, courts-martial, to consist of three commissioned officers, for the trial and punishment of offences not capital, and decide upon their sentences. For the same purposes, all officers commanding any of the garrisons, forts, barracks, or other places where the troops consist of different corps, may assemble courts-martial, to consist of three commissioned officers, and decide upon their sentences.

ART. 67.   No garrison or regimental court-martial shall have the power to try capital cases or commissioned officers; neither shall they inflict a fine exceeding one month's pay, nor imprison, nor put to hard labor, any non-commissioned officer or soldier for a longer time than one month.

---

*ART. 65. *continued*

The proceedings and sentences of said court shall be sent directly to the Secretary of War, to be by him laid before the President, for his confirmation or approval, or orders in the case.

So much of the sixty-fifth article of the first section of "An act for the establishing rules and articles for the government of the armies of the United States," passed on the tenth of April, eighteen hundred and six, as is repugnant hereto, shall be, and the same is hereby, repealed.

ART. 68. Whenever it may be found convenient and necessary to the public service, the officers of the marines shall be associated with the officers of the land forces, for the purpose of holding courts-martial, and trying offenders belonging to either; and, in such cases, the orders of the senior officer of either corps who may be present and duly authorized, shall be received and obeyed.

ART. 69. The judge advocate, or some person deputed by him, or by the general, or officer commanding the army, detachment, or garrison, shall prosecute in the name of the United States, but shall so far consider himself as counsel for the prisoner, after the said prisoner shall have made his plea, as to object to any leading question to any of the witnesses or any question to the prisoner, the answer to which might tend to criminate himself; and administer to each member of the court, before they proceed upon any trial, the following oath, which shall also be taken by all members of the regimental and garrison courts-martial:

"You, A. B., do swear, that you will well and truly try and determine, according to evidence, the matter now before you, between the United States of America and the prisoner to be tried, and that you will duly administer justice, according to the provisions of 'An act establishing Rules and Articles for the government of the armies of the United States,' without partiality, favor, or affection; and if any doubt should arise, not explained by said Articles, according to your conscience, the best of your understanding, and the custom of war in like cases; and you do further swear that you will not divulge the sentence of the court until it shall be published by the proper authority; neither will you disclose or discover the vote or opinion of any particular member of the court-martial, unless required to give evidence thereof, as a witness by a court of justice, in a due course of law. So help you God."

And as soon as the said oath shall have administered to the respective members, the president of the court shall administer to the judge advocate, or person officiating as such, an oath in the following words:

"You, A. B., do swear, you will not disclose or discover the vote or opinion of any particular member of the court-martial, unless required to give evidence thereof, as a witness, by a court of justice, in due course of law; nor divulge the sentence of the court to any but the proper authority, until it shall be duly disclosed by the same. So help you God."

ART. 70.   When a prisoner, arraigned before a general court-martial, shall, from obstinacy and deliberate design, stand mute, or answer foreign to the purpose, the court may proceed to trial and judgment as if the prisoner had regularly pleaded not guilty.

ART. 71.   When a member shall be challenged by a prisoner, be must state his cause of challenge, of which the court shall, after due deliberation, determine the relevancy or validity, and decide accordingly; and no challenge to more than one member at a time shall be received by the court.

ART. 72.   All the members of a court-martial are to behave with decency and calmness; and in giving their votes are to begin with the youngest in commission.

ART. 73.   All persons who give evidence before a court-martial are to be examined on oath of affirmation, in the following form:

"You swear, or affirm (as the cause may be), the evidence you shall give in the cause now in hearing shall be the truth, the whole truth, and nothing but the truth. So help you God."

ART. 74.   On the trials of cases not capital, before courts-martial, the deposition of witnesses, not in the line or staff of the army, may be taken before some justice of the peace, and read in evidence; provided the prosecutor and person accused are present at the taking of the same, or are duly notified thereof.

ART. 75.   No officers shall be tried but by a general court-martial, nor by officers of an inferior rank, if it can be avoided. Nor shall any proceedings of trials be carried on, excepting between the hours of eight in the morning and three in the afternoon, excepting in cases which, in the opinion of the officer appointing the court-martial, require immediate example.

ART. 76.   No person whatsoever shall use any menacing words, signs, or gestures, in presence of a court-martial, or shall cause any disorder or riot, or disturbing their proceedings, on the penalty of being punished at the discretion of the said court-martial.

ART. 77.   Whenever any officer shall be charged with a crime he shall be arrested and confined in his barracks, quarters, or tent, and deprived of his sword by the commanding officer. And any officer who shall leave his confinement before he shall be set at liberty by his commanding officer, or by a superior officer, shall be cashiered.

ART. 78.   Non-commissioned officers and soldiers, charged with crimes, shall be confined until tried by a court-martial, or released by proper authority.

ART. 79.   No officer or soldier who shall be put in arrest shall continue in confinement more than eight days, or until such time as a court-martial can be assembled.

ART. 80.   No officer commanding a guard, or provost marshal, shall refuse to receive or keep any prisoner committed to his charge by an officer belonging to the forces of the United States; provided the officer committing shall, at the same time, deliver an account in writing, signed by himself, of the crime with which the said prisoner is charged.

ART. 81. No officer commanding a guard, or provost marshal, shall presume to release any person committed to his charge without proper authority for so doing, nor shall he suffer any person to escape, on the penalty of being punished for it by the sentence of a court-martial.

ART. 82. Every officer or provost marshal, to whom charge prisoners shall be committed, shall, within twenty-four hours after such commitment, or as soon as he shall be relieved from his guard, make report in writing, to the commanding officer, of their names, their crimes, and the names of the officers who committed them, on the penalty of being punished for disobedience or neglect, at the discretion of a court-martial.

ART. 83. Any commissioned officer convicted before a general court-martial of conduct unbecoming an officer and a gentleman, shall be dismissed the service.

ART. 84. In cases where a court-martial may think it proper to sentence a commissioned officer to be suspended from command, they shall have power also to suspend his pay and emoluments for the same time, according to the nature and heinousness of the offense.

ART. 85. In all cases where a commissioned officer is cashiered for cowardice or fraud, it shall be added in the sentence, that the crime, name, and place of abode, and punishment of the delinquent, be published in the newspapers in and about the camp, and of the particular State from which the offender came, or where he usually resides; after which it shall be deemed scandalous for an officer to associate with him.

ART. 86. The commanding officer of any post or detachment, in which there shall not be a number of officers adequate to form a general court-martial, shall, in cases which require the cognizance of such a court, report to the commanding officer of the department, who shall order a court to be assembled at the nearest post or department, and the party accused, with necessary witnesses, to be transported to the place where the said court shall be assembled.

ART. 87. No person shall be sentenced to suffer death but by the concurrence of two-thirds of the members of a general court-martial, nor except in the cases herein expressly mentioned; *nor shall more than fifty lashes be inflicted on any offender, at the discretion of a court-martial*; and no officer, non-commissioned officer, soldier, or follower of the army shall be tried a second time for the same offense.[*]

ART. 88. No person shall be liable to be tried and punished by a general court-martial for any offense which shall appear to have been committed more than two years before the issuing of the order for such trial, unless the person, by reason of having absented himself, or some other manifested impediment, shall not have been amenable to justice within that period.

ART. 89. Every officer authorized to order a general court-martial shall have power to pardon or mitigate any punishment ordered by such court, except the sentence of death, or of cashiering an officer; which, in the cases where he has authority (by Article 65) to carry them into execution, he may suspend, until the pleasure of the President of the United States can be known; which suspension, together with copies of the proceedings of the court-martial, the said officer shall immediately transmit to the President for his determination. And the colonel or commanding officer of the regiment or garrison where any regimental or garrison court-martial shall be held, may pardon or mitigate any punishment ordered by such court-martial to be inflicted.

---

[*]So much of these rules and articles as authorizes the infliction of corporeal punishment by stripes or lashes, was specially repealed by act of 16th May 1812. By Act of 2d March 1833, the repealed act was itself repealed, so far as it applied to the crime of desertion, which, of course, revived the punishment by lashes for that offense. Flogging was totally abolished by Sec. 3 of Chap. 54, 5 August, 1861.

ART. 90.   Every judge advocate, or person officiating as such, at any general court-martial, shall transmit, with as much expedition as the opportunity of the time and distance of place can admit, the original proceedings and sentence of such court-martial to the Secretary of War; which said original proceedings and sentence shall be carefully kept and preserved in the office of said Secretary, to the end that the persons entitled thereto may be enabled, upon application to the said office, to obtain copies thereof.

The party tried by any general court-martial shall, upon demand thereof, made by himself, or by any person or persons in his behalf, be entitled to a copy of the sentence and proceedings of such court-martial.

ART. 91.   In cases where the general, or commanding officer may order a court of inquiry to examine into the nature of any transaction, accusation, or imputation against any officer or soldier, the said court shall consist of one or more officers, not exceeding three, and a judge advocate, or other suitable person, as a recorder, to reduce the proceedings and evidence to writing; all of whom shall be sworn to the faithful performance of their duty. This court shall have the same power to summon witnesses as a court-martial, and to examine them on oath. But they shall not give their opinion on the merits of the case, excepting they shall be thereto specially required. The parties accused shall also be permitted to cross-examine and interrogate the witness, so as to investigate fully the circumstances in the question.

ART. 92.   The proceedings of a court of inquiry must be authenticated by the signatures of the recorder and the president, and delivered to the commanding officer, and the said proceedings may be admitted as evidence by a court-martial, in cases not capital or extending to the dismission of an officer, provided that the circumstances are such that oral testimony cannot be obtained. But as courts of inquiry may be perverted to dishonorable purposes, and may be considered as engines of destruction to military merit, in the hands of weak and envious commandants, they are hereby prohibited, unless directed by the President of the United States, or demanded by the accused.

ART. 93.   The judge advocate or recorder shall administer to the members the following oath:

"You shall well and truly examine and inquire, according to your evidence, into the matter now before you, without partiality, favor, affection, prejudice, or hope of reward. So help you God."

After which the president shall administer to the judge advocate or recorder the following oath:

"You, A. B., do swear that you will according to your best abilities accurately and impartially record the proceedings of the court, and the evidence to be given in the case in hearing. So help you God."

The witnesses shall take the same oath as witnesses sworn before a court-martial.

ART. 94.   When any commissioned officer shall die or be killed in the service of the United States, the major of the regiment, or the officer doing the major's duty in his absence, or in any post or garrison, the second officer in command, or the assistant military agent, shall immediately secure all his effects or equipage, then in camp or quarters, and shall make an inventory thereof, and forthwith transmit the same to the office of the Department of War, to the end that his executors or administrators may receive the same.

ART. 95.   When any non-commissioned officer or soldier shall die, or be killed in the service of the United States, the then commanding officer of the troop or company shall, in the presence of two other commissioned officers, take an account of what effects he died possessed of, above his arms and accoutrements, and transmit the same to the office of the Department of War, which said effects are to be accounted for, and paid to the representatives of such deceased non-commissioned officer or soldier. And in case any of the officers, so authorized to take care of the effects of deceased officers and soldiers, should, before they have accounted to their representatives for the same, have occasion to leave the regiment or post, for preferment or otherwise, they shall, before they be permitted to quit the same, deposit in the hands of the commanding officer, or of the assistant military agent, all the effects of such deceased non-commissioned officers and soldiers, in order that the same may be secured for, and paid to, their respective representatives.

ART. 96.   All officers, conductors, gunners, matrosses, drivers, or other persons whatsoever, receiving pay or hire in the service of the artillery, or corps of engineers of the United States, shall be governed by the aforesaid Rules and Articles, and shall be subject to be tried by courts-martial, in like manner with the officers and soldiers of the other troops in the service of the United States.

ART. 97.   The officers and soldiers of any troops, whether militia or others, being mustered out in pay of the United States, shall, at all times and in all places, when joined or acting in conjunction with the regular forces of the United States, be governed by these rules and articles of war, and shall be subject to be tried by courts-martial, in like manner with the officers and soldiers in the regular forces; save only that such courts-martial shall be composed entirely of militia officers.

ART. 98.   All officers serving by commission from the authority of any particular State, shall, on all detachments, courts-martial, or other duty, wherein they may be employed in conjunction with the regular forces of the United States, take rank next after all officers of the like grade in said regular forces, notwithstanding the commission of such militia or State officers may be elder than the commissions of the officers of the regular forces of the United States.

ART. 99.   All crimes not capital, and all disorders and neglects which officers and soldiers may be guilty of, to the prejudice of good order and military discipline, though not mentioned in the foregoing articles of war, are to be taken cognizance of by a general or regimental court-martial, according to the nature and degree of the offense, and be punished at their discretion.

ART. 100. The President of the United States shall have power to prescribe the uniform of the army.

ART. ———. All officers or persons in the military or naval service of the United States are prohibited from employing any of the forces under their respective commands for the purpose of returning fugitives from service or labor, who may have escaped from any persons to whom such labor or service is claimed to be due; and any officer who shall be found guilty by a court-martial of violating this article shall be dismissed from the service.[*]

ART. 101. The foregoing articles are to be read and published, once in every six months, to every garrison, regiment, troop, or company, mustered, or to be mustered, in the service of the United States, and are to be duly observed and obeyed by all officers and soldiers who are, or shall be, in said service.

SECTION II. *And be it further enacted,* That in time of war, all persons not citizens of, or owing allegiance to, the United States of America, who shall be found lurking as spies in or about the fortifications or encampments of the armies of the United States, or any of them, shall suffer death, according to the law and usage of nations, by sentence of a general court-martial.

---

[*]*Approved March 13, 1862 by Act of Congress.* [This article was apparently not numbered as of July 25, 1863, but appears in "Extracts from Acts of Congress" as an approved addition to the *Articles of War.* Ed.]

SECTION III. *And be it further enacted,* That the rules and regulations by which the armies of the United States have heretofore been governed, and the resolves of Congress thereunto annexed, and respecting the same, shall henceforth be void and of no effect, except so far as may relate to any transactions under them prior to the promulgation of this act, at the several posts and garrisons respectively, occupied by any part of the army of the United States. [APPROVED, April 10, 1806.]

PART II.

GENERAL ORDERS No. 100: INSTRUCTIONS FOR THE GOVERNMENT OF THE ARMIES OF THE UNITED STATES IN THE FIELD, APRIL 24, 1863

INSTRUCTIONS

FOR THE

GOVERNMENT OF ARMIES

OF

THE UNITED STATES

IN THE FIELD.

PREPARED BY

FRANCIS LIEBER, LL.D.

U.S. WAR DEPARTMENT

ORIGINALLY ISSUED AS GENERAL ORDERS No. 100,

ADJUTANT GENERAL'S OFFICE, 1863.

WASHINGTON:

GOVERNMENT PRINTING OFFICE.

GENERAL ORDERS,　　　　WAR DEPARTMENT,
　　　　　　　　　　　　ADJUTANT GENERAL'S OFFICE
　No. 100.　　　　　　*Washington, April 24, 1863*

The following "Instructions for the Government of Armies of the United States in the Field," prepared by FRANCIS LIEBER, LL.D., and revised by a Board of Officers, of which Major General E. A. Hitchcock is president, having been approved by the President of the United States, he commands that they be published for the information of all concerned.

BY ORDER OF THE SECRETARY OF WAR:

E. D. TOWNSEND,
Assistant Adjutant General.

INSTRUCTIONS FOR THE GOVERNMENT OF THE ARMIES OF THE UNITED STATES IN THE FIELD.

SECTION I.

Martial Law—Military jurisdiction—Military necessity—Retaliation.

1.

A place, district, or country occupied by an enemy stands, in consequence of the occupation, under the Martial Law of the invading or occupying army, whether any proclamation declaring Martial Law, or any public warning to the inhabitants, has been issued or not. Martial Law is the immediate and direct effect and consequence of occupation or conquest.

The presence of a hostile army proclaims its Martial Law.

2.

Martial Law does not cease during the hostile occupation, except by special proclamation, ordered by the commander in chief; or by special mention in the treaty of peace concluding the war, when the occupation of a place or territory continues beyond the conclusion of peace as one of the conditions of the same.

3.

Martial Law in a hostile country consists in the suspension, by the occupying military authority, of the criminal and civil law, and of the domestic administration and government in the occupied place or territory, and in the substitution of military rule and force for the same, as well as in the dictation of general laws, as far as military necessity requires this suspension, substitution, or dictation.

The commander of the forces may proclaim that the administration of all civil and penal law shall continue either wholly or in part, as in times of peace, unless otherwise ordered by the military authority.

4.

Martial Law is simply military authority exercised in accordance with the laws and usages of war. Military oppression is not Martial Law; it is the abuse of the power which that law confers. As Martial Law is executed by military force, it is incumbent upon those who administer it to be strictly guided by the principles of justice, honor, and humanity—virtues adorning a soldier even more than other men, for the very reason that he possesses the power of his arms against the unarmed.

5.

Martial Law should be less stringent in places and countries fully occupied and fairly conquered. Much greater severity may be exercised in places or regions where actual hostilities exist, or are expected and must be prepared for. Its most complete sway is allowed—even in the commander's own country—when face to face with the enemy, because of the absolute necessities of the case, and of the paramount duty to defend the country against invasion.

To save the country is paramount to all other considerations.

6.

All civil and penal law shall continue to take its usual course in the enemy's places and territories under Martial Law, unless interrupted or stopped by order of the occupying military power; but all the functions of the hostile government-legislative, executive, or administrative—whether of a general, provincial, or local character, cease under Martial Law, or continue only with the sanction, or, if deemed necessary, the participation of the occupier or invader.

7.

Martial Law extends to property, and to persons, whether they are subjects of the enemy or aliens to that government.

8.

Consuls, among American and European nations, are not diplomatic agents. Nevertheless, their offices and persons will be subjected to Martial Law in cases of urgent necessity only: their property and business are not exempted. Any delinquency they commit against the established military rule may be punished as in the case of any other inhabitant, and such punishment furnishes no reasonable ground for international complaint.

9.

The functions of Ambassadors, Ministers, or other diplomatic agents accredited by neutral powers to the hostile government, cease, so far as regards the displaced government; but the conquering or occupying power usually recognizes them as temporarily accredited to itself.

10.

Martial Law affects chiefly the police and collection of public revenue and taxes, whether imposed by the expelled government or by the invader, and refers mainly to the support and efficiency of the army, its safety, and the safety of its operations.

11.

The law of war does not only disclaim all cruelty and bad faith concerning engagements concluded with the enemy during the war, but also the breaking of stipulations solemnly contracted by the belligerents in time of peace, and avowedly intended to remain in force in case of war between the contracting powers.

It disclaims all extortions and other transactions for individual gain; all acts of private revenge, or connivance at such acts.

Offenses to the contrary shall be severely punished, and especially so if committed by officers.

12.

Whenever feasible, Martial Law is carried out in cases of individual offenders by Military Courts; but sentences of death shall be executed only with the approval of the chief executive, provided the urgency of the case does not require a speedier execution, and then only with the approval of the chief commander.

13.

Military jurisdiction is of two kinds: First, that which is conferred and defined by statute; second, that which is derived from the common law of war. Military offenses under the statute law must be tried in the manner therein directed; but military offenses which do not come within the statute must be tried and punished under the common law of war. The character of the courts which exercise these jurisdictions depends upon the local laws of each particular country.

In the armies of the United States the first is exercised by courts-martial, while cases which do not come within the "Rules and Articles of War," or the jurisdiction conferred by statute on courts-martial, are tried by military commissions.

14.

Military necessity, as understood by modern civilized nations, consists in the necessity of those measures which are indispensable for securing the ends of the war, and which are lawful according to the modern law and usages of war.

15.

Military necessity admits of all direct destruction of life or limb of *armed* enemies, and of other persons whose destruction is incidentally *unavoidable* in the armed contests of the war; it allows of the capturing of every armed enemy, and every enemy of importance to the hostile government, or of peculiar danger to the captor; it allows of all destruction of property, and obstruction of the ways and channels of traffic, travel, or communication, and of all withholding of sustenance or means of life from the enemy; of the appropriation of whatever an enemy's country affords necessary for the subsistence and safety of the army, and of such deception as does not involve the breaking of good faith either positively pledged, regarding agreements entered into during the war, or supposed by the modern law of war to exist. Men who take up arms against one another in public war do not cease on this account to be moral beings, responsible to one another and to God.

16.

Military necessity does not admit of cruelty—that is, the infliction of suffering for the sake of suffering or for revenge, nor of maiming or wounding except in fight, nor of torture to extort confessions. It does not admit of the use of poison in any way, nor of the wanton devastation of a district. It admits of deception, but disclaims acts of perfidy; and, in general, military necessity does not include any act of hostility which makes the return to peace unnecessarily difficult.

17.

War is not carried on by arms alone. It is lawful to starve the hostile belligerent, armed or unarmed, so that it leads to the speedier subjection of the enemy.

18.

When a commander of a besieged place expels the noncombatants, in order to lessen the number of those who consume his stock of provisions, it is lawful, though an extreme measure, to drive them back, so as to hasten on the surrender.

19.

Commanders, whenever admissible, inform the enemy of their intention to bombard a place, so that the noncombatants, and especially the women and children, may be removed before the bombardment commences. But it is no infraction of the common law of war to omit thus to inform the enemy. Surprise may be a necessity.

20.

Public war is a state of armed hostility between sovereign nations or governments. It is a law and requisite of civilized existence that men live in political, continuous societies, forming organized units, called states or nations, whose constituents bear, enjoy, and suffer, advance and retrograde together, in peace and in war.

21.

The citizen or native of a hostile country is thus an enemy, as one of the constituents of the hostile state or nation, and as such is subjected to the hardships of the war.

22.

Nevertheless, as civilization has advanced during the last centuries, so has likewise steadily advanced, especially in war on land, the distinction between the private individual belonging to a hostile country and the hostile country itself, with its men in arms. The principle has been more and more acknowledged that the unarmed citizen is to be spared in person, property, and honor as much as the exigencies of war will admit.

23.

Private citizens are no longer murdered, enslaved, or carried off to distant parts, and the inoffensive individual is as little disturbed in his private relations as the commander of the hostile troops can afford to grant in the overruling demands of a vigorous war.

24.

The almost universal rule in remote times was, and continues to be with barbarous armies, that the private individual of the hostile country is destined to suffer every privation of liberty and protection, and every disruption of family ties. Protection was, and still is with uncivilized people, the exception.

25.

In modern regular wars of the Europeans, and their descendants in other portions of the globe, protection of the inoffensive citizen of the hostile country is the rule; privation and disturbance of private relations are the exceptions.

26.

Commanding generals may cause the magistrates and civil officers of the hostile country to take the oath of temporary allegiance or an oath of fidelity to their own victorious government or rulers, and they may expel everyone who declines to do so. But whether they do so or not, the people and their civil officers owe strict obedience to them as long as they hold sway over the district or country, at the peril of their lives.

27.

The law of war can no more wholly dispense with retaliation than can the law of nations, of which it is a branch. Yet civilized nations acknowledge retaliation as the sternest feature of war. A reckless enemy often leaves to his opponent no other means of securing himself against the repetition of barbarous outrage.

28.

Retaliation will, therefore, never be resorted to as a measure of mere revenge, but only as a means of protective retribution, and moreover, cautiously and unavoidably; that is to say, retaliation shall only be resorted to after careful inquiry into the real occurrence, and the character of the misdeeds that may demand retribution.

Unjust or inconsiderate retaliation removes the belligerents farther and farther from the mitigating rules of regular war, and by rapid steps leads them nearer to the internecine wars of savages.

29.

Modern times are distinguished from earlier ages by the existence, at one and the same time, of many nations and great governments related to one another in close intercourse.

Peace is their normal condition; war is the exception. The ultimate object of all modern war is a renewed state of peace.

The more vigorously wars are pursued, the better it is for humanity. Sharp wars are brief.

30.

Ever since the formation and coexistence of modern nations, and ever since wars have become great national wars, war has come to be acknowledged not to be its own end, but the means to obtain great ends of state, or to consist in defense against wrong; and no conventional restriction of the modes adopted to injure the enemy is any longer admitted; but the law of war imposes many limitations and restrictions on principles of justice, faith, and honor.

SECTION II.

Public and private property of the enemy—Protection of persons, and especially of women, of religion, the arts and sciences— Punishment of crimes against the inhabitants of hostile countries.

31.

A victorious army appropriates all public money, seizes all public movable property until further direction by its government, and sequesters for its own benefit or of that of its government all the revenues of real property belonging to the hostile government or nation. The title to such real property remains in abeyance during military occupation, and until the conquest is made complete.

32.

A victorious army, by the martial power inherent in the same, may suspend, change, or abolish, as far as the martial power extends, the relations which arise from the services due, according to the existing laws of the invaded country, from one citizen, subject, or native of the same to another.

The commander of the army must leave it to the ultimate treaty of peace to settle the permanency of this change.

33.

It is no longer considered lawful—on the contrary, it is held to be a serious breach of the law of war—to force the subjects of the enemy into the service of the victorious government, except the latter should proclaim, after a fair and complete conquest of the hostile country or district, that it is resolved to keep the country, district, or place permanently as its own and make it a portion of its own country.

34.

As a general rule, the property belonging to churches, to hospitals, or other establishments of an exclusively charitable character, to establishments of education, or foundations for the promotion of knowledge, whether public schools, universities, academies of learning or observatories, museums of the fine arts, or of a scientific character—such property is not to be considered public property in the sense of paragraph 31; but it may be taxed or used when the public service may require it.

35.

Classical works of art, libraries, scientific collections, or precious instruments, such as astronomical telescopes, as well as hospitals, must be secured against all avoidable injury, even when they are contained in fortified places whilst besieged or bombarded.

36.

If such works of art, libraries, collections, or instruments belonging to a hostile nation or government, can be removed without injury, the ruler of the conquering state or nation may order them to be seized and removed for the benefit of the said nation. The ultimate ownership is to be settled by the ensuing treaty of peace.

In no case shall they be sold or given away, if captured by the armies of the United States, nor shall they ever be privately appropriated, or wantonly destroyed or injured.

37.

The United States acknowledge and protect, in hostile countries occupied by them, religion and morality; strictly private property; the persons of the inhabitants, especially those of women; and the sacredness of domestic relations. Offenses to the contrary shall be rigorously punished.

This rule does not interfere with the right of the victorious invader to tax the people or their property, to levy forced loans, to billet soldiers, or to appropriate property, especially houses, lands, boats or ships, and churches, for temporary and military uses.

38.

Private property, unless forfeited by crimes or by offenses of the owner, can be seized only by way of military necessity, for the support or other benefit of the army or of the United States.

If the owner has not fled, the commanding officer will cause receipts to be given, which may serve the spoliated owner to obtain indemnity.

39.

The salaries of civil officers of the hostile government who remain in the invaded territory, and continue the work of their office, and can continue it according to the circumstances arising out of the war—such as judges, administrative or police officers, officers of city or communal governments—are paid from the public revenue of the invaded territory, until the military government has reason wholly or partially to discontinue it. Salaries or incomes connected with purely honorary titles are always stopped.

40.

There exists no law or body of authoritative rules of action between hostile armies, except that branch of the law of nature and nations which is called the law and usages of war on land.

41.

All municipal law of the ground on which the armies stand, or of the countries to which they belong, is silent and of no effect between armies in the field.

42.

Slavery, complicating and confounding the ideas of property, (that is of a *thing*,) and of personality, (that is of *humanity*,) exists according to municipal or local law only. The law of nature and nations has never acknowledged it. The digest of the Roman law enacts the early dictum of the pagan jurist, that "so far as the law of nature is concerned, all men are equal." Fugitives escaping from a country in which they were slaves, villains, or serfs, into another country, have, for centuries past, been held free and acknowledged free by judicial decisions of European countries, even though the municipal law of the country in which the slave had taken refuge acknowledged slavery within its own dominions.

43.

Therefore, in a war between the United States and a belligerent which admits of slavery, if a person held in bondage by that belligerent be captured by or come as a fugitive under the protection of the military forces of the United States, such person is immediately entitled to the rights and privileges of a freeman. To return such person into slavery would amount to enslaving a free person, and neither the United States nor any officer under their authority can enslave any human being. Moreover, a person so made free by the law of war is under the shield of the law of nations, and the former owner or State can have, by the law of postliminy, no belligerent lien or claim of service.

44.

All wanton violence committed against persons in the invaded country, all destruction of property not commanded by the authorized officer, all robbery, all pillage or sacking, even after taking a place by main force, all rape, wounding, maiming, or killing of such inhabitants, are prohibited under the penalty of death, or such other severe punishment as may seem adequate for the gravity of the offense.

A soldier, officer or private, in the act of committing such violence, and disobeying a superior ordering him to abstain from it, may be lawfully killed on the spot by such superior.

45.

All captures and booty belong, according to the modern law of war, primarily to the government of the captor.

Prize money, whether on sea or land, can now only be claimed under local law.

46.

Neither officers nor soldiers are allowed to make use of their position or power in the hostile country for private gain, not even for commercial transactions otherwise legitimate. Offenses to the contrary committed by commissioned officers will be punished with cashiering or such other punishment as the nature of the offense may require; if by soldiers, they shall be punished according to the nature of the offense.

47.

Crimes punishable by all penal codes, such as arson, murder, maiming, assaults, highway robbery, theft, burglary, fraud, forgery, and rape, if committed by an American soldier in a hostile country against its inhabitants, are not only punishable as at home, but in all cases in which death is not inflicted, the severer punishment shall be preferred.

SECTION III.

Deserters—Prisoners of war—Hostages— Booty on the battle-field.

48.

Deserters from the American Army, having entered the service of the enemy, suffer death if they fall again into the hands of the United States, whether by capture, or being delivered up to the American Army; and if a deserter from the enemy, having taken service in the Army of the United States, is captured by the enemy, and punished by them with death or otherwise, it is not a breach against the law and usages of war, requiring redress or retaliation.

49.

A prisoner of war is a public enemy armed or attached to the hostile army for active aid, who has fallen into the hands of the captor, either fighting or wounded, on the field or in the hospital, by individual surrender or by capitulation.

All soldiers, of whatever species of arms; all men who belong to the rising *en masse* of the hostile country; all those who are attached to the army for its efficiency and promote directly the object of the war, except such as are hereinafter provided for; all disabled men or officers on the field or elsewhere, if captured; all enemies who have thrown away their arms and ask for quarter, are prisoners of war, and as such exposed to the inconveniences as well as entitled to the privileges of a prisoner of war.

50.

Moreover, citizens who accompany an army for whatever purpose, such as sutlers, editors, or reporters of journals, or contractors, if captured, may be made prisoners of war, and be detained as such.

The monarch and members of the hostile reigning family, male or female, the chief, and chief officers of the hostile government, its diplomatic agents, and all persons who are of particular and singular use and benefit to the hostile army or its government, are, if captured on belligerent ground, and if unprovided with a safe conduct granted by the captor's government, prisoners of war.

51.

If the people of that portion of an invaded country which is not yet occupied by the enemy, or of the whole country, at the approach of a hostile army, rise, under a duly authorized levy *en masse* to resist the invader, they are now treated as public enemies, and, if captured, are prisoners of war.

52.

No belligerent has the right to declare that he will treat every captured man in arms of a levy *en masse* as a brigand or bandit.

If, however, the people of a country, or any portion of the same, already occupied by an army, rise against it, they are violators of the laws of war, and are not entitled to their protection.

53.

The enemy's chaplains, officers of the medical staff, apothecaries, hospital nurses and servants, if they fall into the hands of the American Army, are not prisoners of war, unless the commander has reasons to retain them. In this latter case, or if, at their own desire, they are allowed to remain with their captured companions, they are treated as prisoners of war, and may be exchanged if the commander sees fit.

54.

A hostage is a person accepted as a pledge for the fulfillment of an agreement concluded between belligerents during the war, or in consequence of a war. Hostages are rare in the present age.

55.

If a hostage is accepted, he is treated like a prisoner of war, according to rank and condition, as circumstances may admit.

56.

A prisoner of war is subject to no punishment for being a public enemy, nor is any revenge wreaked upon him by the intentional infliction of any suffering, or disgrace, by cruel imprisonment, want of food, by mutilation, death, or any other barbarity.

57.

So soon as a man is armed by a sovereign government and takes the soldier's oath of fidelity, he is a belligerent; his killing, wounding, or other warlike acts are not individual crimes or offenses. No belligerent has a right to declare that enemies of a certain class, color, or condition, when properly organized as soldiers, will not be treated by him as public enemies.

58.

The law of nations knows of no distinction of color, and if an enemy of the United States should enslave and sell any captured persons of their army, it would be a case for the severest retaliation, if not redressed upon complaint.

The United States can not retaliate by enslavement; therefore death must be the retaliation for this crime against the law of nations.

59.

A prisoner of war remains answerable for his crimes committed against the captor's army or people, committed before he was captured, and for which he has not been punished by his own authorities.

All prisoners of war are liable to the infliction of retaliatory measures.

60.

It is against the usage of modern war to resolve, in hatred and revenge, to give no quarter. No body of troops has the right to declare that it will not give, and therefore will not expect, quarter; but a commander is permitted to direct his troops to give no quarter, in great straits, when his own salvation makes it *impossible* to cumber himself with prisoners.

61.

Troops that give no quarter have no right to kill enemies already disabled on the ground, or prisoners captured by other troops.

62.

All troops of the enemy known or discovered to give no quarter in general, or to any portion of the army, receive none.

63.

Troops who fight in the uniform of their enemies, without any plain, striking, and uniform mark of distinction of their own, can expect no quarter.

64.

If American troops capture a train containing uniforms of the enemy, and the commander considers it advisable to distribute them for use among his men, some striking mark or sign must be adopted to distinguish the American soldier from the enemy.

65.

The use of the enemy's national standard, flag, or other emblem of nationality, for the purpose of deceiving the enemy in battle, is an act of perfidy by which they lose all claim to the protection of the laws of war.

66.

Quarter having been given to an enemy by American troops, under a misapprehension of his true character, he may, nevertheless, be ordered to suffer death if, within three days after the battle, it be discovered that he belongs to a corps which gives no quarter.

67.

The law of nations allows every sovereign government to make war upon another sovereign state, and, therefore, admits of no rules or laws different from those of regular warfare, regarding the treatment of prisoners of war, although they may belong to the army of a government which the captor may consider as a wanton and unjust assailant.

68.

Modern wars are not internecine wars, in which the killing of the enemy is the object. The destruction of the enemy in modern war, and, indeed, modern war itself, are means to obtain that object of the belligerent which lies beyond the war.

Unnecessary or revengeful destruction of life is not lawful.

69.

Outposts, sentinels, or pickets are not to be fired upon, except to drive them in, or when a positive order, special or general, has been issued to that effect.

70.

The use of poison in any manner, be it to poison wells, or food, or arms, is wholly excluded from modern warfare. He that uses it puts himself out of the pale of the law and usages of war.

71.

Whoever intentionally inflicts additional wounds on an enemy already wholly disabled, or kills such an enemy, or who orders or encourages soldiers to do so, shall suffer death, if duly convicted, whether he belongs to the Army of the United States, or is an enemy captured after having committed his misdeed.

72.

Money and other valuables on the person of a prisoner, such as watches or jewelry, as well as extra clothing, are regarded by the American Army as the private property of the prisoner, and the appropriation of such valuables or money is considered dishonorable, and is prohibited.

Nevertheless, if *large* sums are found upon the persons of prisoners, or in their possession, they shall be taken from them, and the surplus, after providing for their own support, appropriated for the use of the army, under the direction of the commander, unless otherwise ordered by the government. Nor can prisoners claim, as private property, large sums found and captured in their train, although they have been placed in the private luggage of the prisoners.

73.

All officers, when captured, must surrender their side arms to the captor. They may be restored to the prisoner in marked cases, by the commander, to signalize admiration of his distinguished bravery or approbation of his humane treatment of prisoners before his capture. The captured officer to whom they may be restored can not wear them during captivity.

74.

A prisoner of war, being a public enemy, is the prisoner of the government, and not of the captor. No ransom can be paid by a prisoner of war to his individual captor or to any officer in command. The government alone releases captives, according to rules prescribed by itself.

75.

Prisoners of war are subject to confinement or imprisonment such as may be deemed necessary on account of safety, but they are to be subjected to no other intentional suffering or indignity. The confinement and mode of treating a prisoner may be varied during his captivity according to the demands of safety.

76.

Prisoners of war shall be fed upon plain and wholesome food, whenever practicable, and treated with humanity.

They may be required to work for the benefit of the captor's government, according to their rank and condition.

77.

A prisoner of war who escapes may be shot or otherwise killed in his flight; but neither death nor any other punishment shall be inflicted upon him simply for his attempt to escape, which the law of war does not consider a crime. Stricter means of security shall be used after an unsuccessful attempt at escape.

If, however, a conspiracy is discovered, the purpose of which is a united or general escape, the conspirators may be rigorously punished, even with death; and capital punishment may also be inflicted upon prisoners of war discovered to have plotted rebellion against the authorities of the captors, whether in union with fellow prisoners or other persons.

78.

If prisoners of war, having given no pledge nor made any promise on their honor, forcibly or otherwise escape, and are captured again in battle after having rejoined their own army, they shall not be punished for their escape, but shall be treated as simple prisoners of war, although they will be subjected to stricter confinement.

79.

Every captured wounded enemy shall be medically treated, according to the ability of the medical staff.

80.

Honorable men, when captured, will abstain from giving to the enemy information concerning their own army, and the modern law of war permits no longer the use of any violence against prisoners in order to extort the desired information or to punish them for having given false information.

SECTION IV.

Partisans—Armed enemies not belonging to the hostile army— Scouts—Armed prowlers—War-rebels.

81.

Partisans are soldiers armed and wearing the uniform of their army, but belonging to a corps which acts detached from the main body for the purpose of making inroads into the territory occupied by the enemy. If captured, they are entitled to all the privileges of the prisoner of war.

82.

Men, or squads of men, who commit hostilities, whether by fighting, or inroads for destruction or plunder, or by raids of any kind, without commission, without being part and portion of the organized hostile army, and without sharing continuously in the war, but who do so with intermitting returns to their homes and avocations, or with the occasional assumption of the semblance of peaceful pursuits, divesting themselves of the character or appearance of soldiers—such men, or squads of men, are not public enemies, and, therefore, if captured, are not entitled to the privileges of prisoners of war, but shall be treated summarily as highway robbers or pirates.

83.

Scouts, or single soldiers, if disguised in the dress of the country or in the uniform of the army hostile to their own, employed in obtaining information, if found within or lurking about the lines of the captor, are treated as spies, and suffer death.

84.

Armed prowlers, by whatever names they may be called, or persons of the enemy's territory, who steal within the lines of the hostile army for the purpose of robbing, killing, or of destroying bridges, roads, or canals, or of robbing or destroying the mail, or of cutting the telegraph wires, are not entitled to the privileges of the prisoner of war.

85.

War-rebels are persons within an occupied territory who rise in arms against the occupying or conquering army, or against the authorities established by the same. If captured, they may suffer death, whether they rise singly, in small or large bands, and whether called upon to do so by their own, but expelled, government or not. They are not prisoners of war; nor are they if discovered and secured before their conspiracy has matured to an actual rising or armed violence.

SECTION V.

Safe-conduct—Spies—War-traitors—Captured messengers—Abuse of the flag of truce.

86.

All intercourse between the territories occupied by belligerent armies, whether by traffic, by letter, by travel, or in any other way, ceases. This is the general rule, to be observed without special proclamation.

Exceptions to this rule, whether by safe-conduct, or permission to trade on a small or large scale, or by exchanging mails, or by travel from one territory into the other, can take place only according to agreement approved by the government, or by the highest military authority.

Contraventions of this rule are highly punishable.

87.

Ambassadors, and all other diplomatic agents of neutral powers, accredited to the enemy, may receive safe-conducts through the territories occupied by the belligerents, unless there are military reasons to the contrary, and unless they may reach the place of their destination conveniently by another route. It implies no international affront if the safe-conduct is declined. Such passes are usually given by the supreme authority of the State, and not by subordinate officers.

88.

A spy is a person who secretly, in disguise or under false pretense, seeks information with the intention of communicating it to the enemy. The spy is punishable with death by hanging by the neck, whether or not he succeed in obtaining the information or in conveying it to the enemy.

89.

If a citizen of the United States obtains information in a legitimate manner, and betrays it to the enemy, be he a military or civil officer, or a private citizen, he shall suffer death.

90.

A traitor under the law of war, or a war-traitor, is a person in a place or district under martial law who, unauthorized by the military commander, gives information of any kind to the enemy, or holds intercourse with him.

91.

The war-traitor is always severely punished. If his offense consists in betraying to the enemy anything concerning the condition, safety, operations, or plans of the troops holding or occupying the place or district, his punishment is death.

92.

If the citizen or subject of a country or place invaded or conquered gives information to his own government, from which he is separated by the hostile army, or to the army of his government, he is a war-traitor, and death is the penalty of his offense.

93.

All armies in the field stand in need of guides, and impress them if they can not obtain them otherwise.

94.

No person having been forced by the enemy to serve as guide is punishable for having done so.

95.

If a citizen of a hostile and invaded district voluntarily serves as a guide to the enemy, or offers to do so, he is deemed a war-traitor, and shall suffer death.

96.

A citizen serving voluntarily as a guide against his own country commits treason, and will be dealt with according to the law of his country.

97.

Guides, when it is clearly proved that they have misled intentionally, may be put to death.

98.

An unauthorized or secret communication with the enemy is considered treasonable by the law of war.

Foreign residents in an invaded or occupied territory, or foreign visitors in the same, can claim no immunity from this law. They may communicate with foreign parts, or with the inhabitants of the hostile country, so far as the military authority permits, but no further. Instant expulsion from the occupied territory would be the very least punishment for the infraction of this rule.

99.

A messenger carrying written dispatches or verbal messages from one portion of the army, or from a besieged place, to another portion of the same army, or its government, if armed, and in the uniform of his army, and if captured, while doing so, in the territory occupied by the enemy, is treated by the captor as a prisoner of war. If not in uniform, nor a soldier, the circumstances connected with his capture must determine the disposition that shall be made of him.

100.

A messenger or agent who attempts to steal through the territory occupied by the enemy, to further, in any manner, the interests of the enemy, if captured, is not entitled to the privileges of the prisoner of war, and may be dealt with according to the circumstances of the case.

101.

While deception in war is admitted as a just and necessary means of hostility, and is consistent with honorable warfare, the common law of war allows even capital punishment for clandestine or treacherous attempts to injure an enemy, because they are so dangerous, and it is difficult to guard against them.

102.

The law of war, like the criminal law regarding other offenses, makes no difference on account of the difference of sexes, concerning the spy, the war-traitor, or the war-rebel.

103.

Spies, war-traitors, and war-rebels are not exchanged according to the common law of war. The exchange of such persons would require a special cartel, authorized by the government, or, at a great distance from it, by the chief commander of the army in the field.

104.

A successful spy or war-traitor, safely returned to his own army, and afterwards captured as an enemy, is not subject to punishment for his acts as a spy or war-traitor, but he may be held in closer custody as a person individually dangerous.

SECTION VI.

Exchange of prisoners—Flags of truce—Flags of protection.

105.

Exchanges of prisoners take place—number for number—rank for rank—wounded for wounded—with added condition for added condition—such, for instance, as not to serve for a certain period.

106.

In exchanging prisoners of war, such numbers of persons of inferior rank may be substituted as an equivalent for one of superior rank as may be agreed upon by cartel, which requires the sanction of the government, or of the commander of the army in the field.

107.

A prisoner of war is in honor bound truly to state to the captor his rank; and he is not to assume a lower rank than belongs to him, in order to cause a more advantageous exchange, nor a higher rank, for the purpose of obtaining better treatment.

Offenses to the contrary have been justly punished by the commanders of released prisoners, and may be good cause for refusing to release such prisoners.

108.

The surplus number of prisoners of war remaining after an exchange has taken place is sometimes released either for the payment of a stipulated sum of money, or, in urgent cases, of provision, clothing, or other necessaries.

Such arrangement, however, requires the sanction of the highest authority.

109.

The exchange of prisoners of war is an act of convenience to both belligerents. If no general cartel has been concluded, it cannot be demanded by either of them. No belligerent is obliged to exchange prisoners of war.

A cartel is voidable as soon as either party has violated it.

110.

No exchange of prisoners shall be made except after complete capture, and after an accurate account of them, and a list of the captured officers, has been taken.

111.

The bearer of a flag of truce cannot insist upon being admitted. He must always be admitted with great caution. Unnecessary frequency is carefully to be avoided.

112.

If the bearer of a flag of truce offer himself during an engagement, he can be admitted as a very rare exception only. It is no breach of good faith to retain such flag of truce, if admitted during the engagement. Firing is not required to cease on the appearance of a flag of truce in battle.

113.

If the bearer of a flag of truce, presenting himself during an engagement, is killed or wounded, it furnishes no ground of complaint whatever.

114.

If it be discovered, and fairly proved, that a flag of truce has been abused for surreptitiously obtaining military knowledge, the bearer of the flag thus abusing his sacred character is deemed a spy.

So sacred is the character of a flag of truce, and so necessary is its sacredness, that while its abuse is an especially heinous offense, great caution is requisite, on the other hand, in convicting the bearer of a flag of truce as a spy.

115.

It is customary to designate by certain flags (usually yellow) the hospitals in places which are shelled, so that the besieging enemy may avoid firing on them. The same has been done in battles, when hospitals are situated within the field of the engagement.

116.

Honorable belligerents often request that the hospitals within the territory of the enemy may be designated, so that they may be spared.

An honorable belligerent allows himself to be guided by flags or signals of protection as much as the contingencies and the necessities of the fight will permit.

117.

It is justly considered an act of bad faith, of infamy or fiendishness, to deceive the enemy by flags of protection. Such act of bad faith may be good cause for refusing to respect such flags.

118.

The besieging belligerent has sometimes requested the besieged to designate the buildings containing collections of works of art, scientific museums, astronomical observatories, or precious libraries, so that their destruction may be avoided as much as possible.

SECTION VII.

The Parole.

119.

Prisoners of war may be released from captivity by exchange, and, under certain circumstances, also by parole.

120.

The term Parole designates the pledge of individual good faith and honor to do, or to omit doing, certain acts after he who gives his parole shall have been dismissed, wholly or partially, from the power of the captor.

121.

The pledge of the parole is always an individual, but not a private act.

122.

The parole applies chiefly to prisoners of war whom the captor allows to return to their country, or to live in greater freedom within the captor's country or territory, on conditions stated in the parole.

123.

Release of prisoners of war by exchange is the general rule; release by parole is the exception.

124.

Breaking the parole is punished with death when the person breaking the parole is captured again. Accurate lists, therefore, of the paroled persons must be kept by the belligerents.

125.

When paroles are given and received there must be an exchange of two written documents, in which the name and rank of the paroled individuals are accurately and truthfully stated.

126.

Commissioned officers only are allowed to give their parole, and they can give it only with the permission of their superior, as long as a superior in rank is within reach.

127.

No noncommissioned officer or private can give his parole except through an officer. Individual paroles not given through an officer are not only void, but subject the individuals giving them to the punishment of death as deserters. The only admissible exception is where individuals, properly separated from their commands, have suffered long confinement without the possibility of being paroled through an officer.

128.

No paroling on the battlefield; no paroling of entire bodies of troops after a battle; and no dismissal of large numbers of prisoners, with a general declaration that they are paroled, is permitted, or of any value.

129.

In capitulations for the surrender of strong places or fortified camps the commanding officer, in cases of urgent necessity, may agree that the troops under his command shall not fight again during the war, unless exchanged.

130.

The usual pledge given in the parole is not to serve during the existing war, unless exchanged.

This pledge refers only to the active service in the field, against the paroling belligerent or his allies actively engaged in the same war. These cases of breaking the parole are patent acts, and can be visited with the punishment of death; but the pledge does not refer to internal service, such as recruiting or drilling the recruits, fortifying places not besieged, quelling civil commotions, fighting against belligerents unconnected with the paroling belligerents, or to civil or diplomatic service for which the paroled officer may be employed.

131.

If the government does not approve of the parole, the paroled officer must return into captivity, and should the enemy refuse to receive him, he is free of his parole.

132.

A belligerent government may declare, by a general order, whether it will allow paroling, and on what conditions it will allow it. Such order is communicated to the enemy.

133.

No prisoner of war can be forced by the hostile government to parole himself, and no government is obliged to parole prisoners of war, or to parole all captured officers, if it paroles any. As the pledging of the parole is an individual act, so is paroling, on the other hand, an act of choice on the part of the belligerent.

134.

The commander of an occupying army may require of the civil officers of the enemy, and of its citizens, any pledge he may consider necessary for the safety or security of his army, and upon their failure to give it he may arrest, confine, or detain them.

SECTION VIII.

Armistice—Capitulation.

135.

An armistice is the cessation of active hostilities for a period agreed between belligerents. It must be agreed upon in writing, and duly ratified by the highest authorities of the contending parties.

136.

If an armistice be declared, without conditions, it extends no further than to require a total cessation of hostilities along the front of both belligerents. If conditions be agreed upon, they should be clearly expressed, and must be rigidly adhered to by both parties. If either party violates any express condition, the armistice may be declared null and void by the other.

137.

An armistice may be general, and valid for all points and lines of the belligerents, or special, that is, referring to certain troops or certain localities only.

An armistice may be concluded for a definite time; or for an indefinite time, during which either belligerent may resume hostilities on giving the notice agreed upon to the other.

138.

The motives which induce the one or the other belligerent to conclude an armistice, whether it be expected to be preliminary to a treaty of peace, or to prepare during the armistice for a more vigorous prosecution of the war, does in no way affect the character of the armistice itself.

139.

An armistice is binding upon the belligerents from the day of the agreed commencement; but the officers of the armies are responsible from the day only when they receive official information of its existence.

140.

Commanding officers have the right to conclude armistices binding on the district over which their command extends, but such armistice is subject to the ratification of the superior authority, and ceases so soon as it is made known to the enemy that the armistice is not ratified, even if a certain time for the elapsing between giving notice of cessation and the resumption of hostilities should have been stipulated for.

141.

It is incumbent upon the contracting parties of an armistice to stipulate what intercourse of persons or traffic between the inhabitants of the territories occupied by the hostile armies shall be allowed, if any.

If nothing is stipulated the intercourse remains suspended, as during actual hostilities.

142.

An armistice is not a partial or a temporary peace; it is only the suspension of military operations to the extent agreed upon by the parties.

143.

When an armistice is concluded between a fortified place and the army besieging it, it is agreed by all the authorities on this subject that the besieger must cease all extension, perfection, or advance of his attacking works as much so as from attacks by main force.

But as there is a difference of opinion among martial jurists, whether the besieged have the right to repair breaches or to erect new works of defense within the place during an armistice, this point should be determined by express agreement between the parties.

144.

So soon as a capitulation is signed, the capitulator has no right to demolish, destroy, or injure the works, arms, stores, or ammunition, in his possession, during the time which elapses between the signing and the execution of the capitulation, unless otherwise stipulated in the same.

145.

When an armistice is clearly broken by one of the parties, the other party is released from all obligation to observe it.

146.

Prisoners taken in the act of breaking an armistice must be treated as prisoners of war, the officer alone being responsible who gives the order for such a violation of an armistice. The highest authority of the belligerent aggrieved may demand redress for the infraction of an armistice.

147.

Belligerents sometimes conclude an armistice while their plenipotentiaries are met to discuss the conditions of a treaty of peace; but plenipotentiaries may meet without a preliminary armistice; in the latter case, the war is carried on without any abatement.

SECTION IX.

Assassination.

148.

The law of war does not allow proclaiming either an individual belonging to the hostile army, or a citizen, or a subject of the hostile government, an outlaw, who may be slain without trial by any captor, any more than the modern law of peace allows such intentional outlawry; on the contrary, it abhors such outrage. The sternest retaliation should follow the murder committed in consequence of such proclamation, made by whatever authority. Civilized nations look with horror upon offers of rewards for the assassination of enemies as relapses into barbarism.

SECTION X.

Insurrection—Civil War—Rebellion.

149.

Insurrection is the rising of people in arms against their government, or a portion of it, or against one or more of its laws, or against an officer or officers of the government. It may be confined to mere armed resistance, or it may have greater ends in view.

150.

Civil war is war between two or more portions of a country or state, each contending for the mastery of the whole, and each claiming to be the legitimate government. The term is also sometimes applied to war of rebellion, when the rebellious provinces or portions of the state are contiguous to those containing the seat of government.

151.

The term rebellion is applied to an insurrection of large extent, and is usually a war between the legitimate government of a country and portions of provinces of the same who seek to throw off their allegiance to it and set up a government of their own.

152.

When humanity induces the adoption of the rules of regular war toward rebels, whether the adoption is partial or entire, it does in no way whatever imply a partial or complete acknowledgment of their government, if they have set up one, or of them, as an independent and sovereign power. Neutrals have no right to make the adoption of the rules of war by the assailed government toward rebels the ground of their own acknowledgment of the revolted people as an independent power.

153.

Treating captured rebels as prisoners of war, exchanging them, concluding of cartels, capitulations, or other warlike agreements with them; addressing officers of a rebel army by the rank they may have in the same; accepting flags of truce; or, on the other hand, proclaiming martial law in their territory, or levying war-taxes or forced loans, or doing any other act sanctioned or demanded by the law and usages of public war between sovereign belligerents, neither proves nor establishes an acknowledgment of the rebellious people, or of the government which they may have erected, as a public or sovereign power. Nor does the adoption of the rules of war toward rebels imply an engagement with them extending beyond the limits of these rules. It is victory in the field that ends the strife and settles the future relations between the contending parties.

154.

Treating, in the field, the rebellious enemy according to the law and usages of war has never prevented the legitimate government from trying the leaders of the rebellion or chief rebels for high treason, and from treating them accordingly, unless they are included in a general amnesty.

155.

All enemies in regular war are divided into two general classes—that is to say, into combatants and noncombatants, or unarmed citizens of the hostile government.

The military commander of the legitimate government, in a war of rebellion, distinguishes between the loyal citizen in the revolted portion of the country and the disloyal citizen. The disloyal citizens may further be classified into those citizens known to sympathize with the rebellion without positively aiding it, and those who, without taking up arms, give positive aid and comfort to the rebellious enemy without being bodily forced thereto.

156.

Common justice and plain expediency require that the military commander protect the manifestly loyal citizens, in revolted territories, against the hardships of the war as much as the common misfortune of all war admits.

The commander will throw the burden of the war, as much as lies within his power, on the disloyal citizens, of the revolted portion or province, subjecting them to a stricter police than the noncombatant enemies have to suffer in regular war; and if he deems it appropriate, or if his government demands of him that every citizen shall, by an oath of allegiance, or by some other manifest act, declare his fidelity to the legitimate government, he may expel, transfer, imprison, or fine the revolted citizens who refuse to pledge themselves anew as citizens obedient to the law and loyal to the government.

Whether it is expedient to do so, and whether reliance can be placed upon such oaths, the commander or his government have the right to decide.

157.

Armed or unarmed resistance by citizens of the United States against the lawful movements of their troops is levying war against the United States, and is therefore treason.

PART III.

GENERAL ORDERS 49:
ORDER FOR THE MAKING AND
GRANTING OF PAROLES,
FEBRUARY 28, 1863

ORDER FOR THE MAKING AND GRANTING OF PAROLES

GENERAL ORDERS,   WAR DEPARTMENT,
ADJUTANT GENERAL'S OFFICE
No. 49.   *Washington, February 28, 1863*

SECTION I:

The following rules in regard to paroles established by the common law and usages of war are published for the information of all concerned:

1. Paroling must always take place by the exchange of signed duplicates of a written document in which the name and rank of the parties paroled are correctly stated. Any one who intentionally misstates his rank forfeits the benefit of his parole and is liable to punishment.

2. None but commissioned officers can give the parole for themselves or their commands, and no inferior officer can give a parole without the authority of his superior if within reach.

3. No paroling on the battle-field. No paroling of entire bodies of troops after a battle and no dismissal of large numbers of prisoners with a general declaration that they are paroled is permitted or of any value.

4. An officer who gives a parole for himself or his command on the battle-field is deemed a deserter and will be punished accordingly.

5. For the officer the pledging of his parole is an individual act, and no wholesale paroling by an officer for a number of inferiors in rank is permitted or valid.

6. No non-commissioned officer or private can give his parole except through an officer. Individual paroles not given through an officer are not only void but subject the individuals giving them to the punishment of death as deserters. The only admissible exception is where individuals properly separated from their commands have suffered long confinement without the possibility of being paroled through an officer.

7. No prisoner of war can be forced by the hostile Government to pledge his parole, and any threat or ill-treatment to force the giving of the parole is contrary to the law of war.

8. No prisoner of war can enter into engagements inconsistent with his character and duties as a citizen and a subject of his State. He can only bind himself not to bear arms against his captor for a limited period, or until he is exchanged, and this only with the stipulated or implied consent of his Government. If the engagement which he makes is not approved by his Government he is bound to return and surrender himself as a prisoner of war. His own Government cannot at the same time disown his engagement and refuse his return as a prisoner.

9. No one can pledge his parole that he will never bear arms against the Government of his captors, nor that he will not bear arms against any other enemy of his Government not at the time the ally of his captors. Such agreements have reference only to the existing enemy and his existing allies and to the existing war and not to future belligerents.

10. While the pledging of the military parole is a voluntary act of the individual, the capturing power is not obliged to grant it, nor is the Government of the individual paroled bound to approve or ratify it.

11.   Paroles not authorized by the common law of war are not valid until approved by the Government of the individual so pledging his parole.

12.   The pledging of any unauthorized military parole is a military offense punishable under the common law of war.

SECTION II.

This order will be published at the head of every regiment in the service of the United States and will be officially communicated by every general commanding an army in the field to the commanding general of the opposing forces and will be hereafter strictly observed and enforced in the armies of the United States.[*]

By order of Maj. Gen. H. W. Halleck:

L. Thomas

Adjutant-General

---

[*]This order was published in March 1863 to Benjamin S. Ewell, assistant adjutant-general to Confederate States Lieutenant General Joseph E. Johnston, "for the information of General Johnston's command."

PART IV.

EXTRACTS
OF
REVISED UNITED STATES
ARMY REGULATIONS

EXTRACTS OF REVISED
UNITED STATES
ARMY REGULATIONS

OF

1861.

WITH AN APPENDIX

CONTAINING THE

CHANGES AND LAWS AFFECTING
ARMY REGULATIONS TO JUNE 25, 1863.

WASHINGTON:
GOVERNMENT PRINTING OFFICE.
1863.

WAR DEPARTMENT,
WASHINGTON, AUGUST 10, 1861.

WHEREAS, it has been found expedient to revise the Regulations for the Army, and the same having been approved by the President of the United States, he commands that they be published for the information and government of the military service, and that, from and after the date hereof, they shall be strictly observed as the sole and standing authority upon the matter herein contained.

Nothing contrary to the tenor of these Regulations will be enjoined in any part of the forces of the United States by any commander whatsoever.

SIMON CAMERON,
Secretary of War.

REVISED REGULATIONS
FOR THE ARMY.

ARTICLE I.

MILITARY DISCIPLINE.

1. ALL inferiors are required to obey strictly, and to execute with alacrity and good faith, the lawful orders of the superiors appointed over them.

2. Military authority is to be exercised with firmness, but with kindness and justice to inferiors. Punishments shall be strictly conformable to military law.

3. Superiors of every grade are forbidden to injure those under them by tyrannical or capricious conduct, or by abusive language.

ARTICLE II.

RANK AND COMMAND.

4. Rank of officers and non-commissioned officers:
- 1st.   Lieutenant-General.
- 2d.   Major-General.
- 3d.   Brigadier-General.
- 4th.   Colonel.
- 5th.   Lieutenant-Colonel.
- 6th.   Major.
- 7th.   Captain.
- 8th.   First Lieutenant.
- 9th.   Second Lieutenant.
- 10th.   Cadet.

11th.   Sergeant-Major.

12th.   Quartermaster-Sergeant of a Regiment.

13th.   Ordnance Sergeant and Hospital Steward.

14th.   First Sergeant.

15th.   Sergeant.

16th.   Corporal.

And in each grade by date of commission or appointment.

7. If, upon marches, guards, or in quarters, different corps of the army shall happen to join, or do duty together, the officer highest in rank of the *line* of the army, marine corps, or militia, by commission, there on duty or in quarters, shall command the whole, and give orders for what is needful to the service, unless otherwise specially directed by the President of the United States, according to the nature of the case.—*(62d Art. of War.)*

9. Officers serving *by commission* from any state of the Union take rank next after officers of the like grade *by commission* from the United States.

12. The officers of Engineers are not to assume nor to be ordered on any duty beyond the line of their immediate profession, except by the special order of the President.

13. An officer of the Pay or Medical Department cannot exercise command except in his own department; but, by virtue of their commissions, officers of these departments may command all *enlisted* men, like other commissioned officers.

14. Officers of the corps of Engineers or Ordnance, or of the Adjutant-General's, Inspector-General's, Quartermaster-General's, or Subsistence Department, though eligible to command according to the rank they hold in the army of the United States, shall not assume the command of troops unless put on duty under orders which specially so direct by authority of the President.

ARTICLE III.

SUCCESSION IN COMMAND OR DUTY.

15. The functions assigned to any officer in these regulations by title of office, devolve on the officer acting in his place, except as specially excepted.

17. An officer who succeeds to any command or duty, stands in regard to his duties in the same situation as his predecessor. The officer relieved shall turn over to his successor all orders in force at the time, and all the public property and funds pertaining to his command or duty, and shall receive therefor duplicate receipts, showing the condition of each article.

18. An officer in a temporary command shall not, except in urgent cases, alter or annul the standing orders of the regular or permanent commander without authority from the next higher commander.

ARTICLE IV.

APPOINTMENT AND PROMOTION OF COMMISSIONED OFFICERS.

19. All vacancies in established regiments and corps, to the rank of Colonel, shall be filled by promotion according to seniority, except in case of disability or other incompetency.

20. Promotions to the rank of Captain shall be made regimentally; to Major and Lieutenant-Colonel and Colonel, according to the arm, as infantry, artillery, &c., and in the Staff Departments and in the Engineers, Topographical Engineers, and Ordnance, according to corps.

21. Appointments to the rank of Brigadier-General and Major-General will be made by selection from the army.

22. The graduates of the Military Academy are appointed to vacancies of the lowest grade, or attached by brevet to regiments or corps, not to exceed one brevet to each company; and merito-

rious non-commissioned officers, examined by an Army Board, and found qualified for the duties of commissioned officers, will, in like manner, be attached to regiments as Brevet Second Lieutenants.

23. Whenever the public service may require the appointment of any citizen to the army, a Board of Officers will be instituted, before which the applicant will appear for an examination into his physical ability, moral character, attainments, and general fitness for the service. If the Board report in favor of the applicant, he will be deemed eligible for a commission in the army.

ARTICLE V.

RESIGNATIONS OF OFFICERS.

24. No officer will be considered out of service on the tender of his resignation, until it shall have been duly accepted by the proper authority. Any officer who, having tendered his resignation, shall, prior to due notice of the acceptance of the same by the proper authority, and, without leave, quit his post or proper duties with the intent to remain permanently absent therefrom, shall be registered as a deserter, and punished as such.

26. Resignations tendered under charges, when forwarded by any commander, will always be accompanied by a copy of the charges; or, in the absence of written charges, by a report of the case, for the information of the Secretary of War.

ARTICLE VI.

EXCHANGE OR TRANSFER OF OFFICERS.

30. The transfer of officers from one regiment or corps to another will be made only by the War Department, on the mutual application of the parties desiring the exchange.

31. An officer shall not be transferred from one regiment or corps to another with prejudice to the rank of any officer of the regiment or corps to which he is transferred.

32. Transfers will be seldom granted—never except for cogent reasons.

ARTICLE VII.

APPOINTMENTS ON THE STAFF.

33. As far as practicable, all appointments and details on the staff will be equalized among the several regiments.

34. General Officers appoint their own Aides-de-camp.

37. An officer of a mounted corps shall not be separated from his regiment, except for duty connected with his particular arm.

38. The senior Lieutenant present, holding the appointment of Assistant Commissary of Subsistence, is entitled to perform the duties.

ARTICLE VIII.

DISTRIBUTION OF THE TROOPS.

39. The military geographical departments will be established by the War Department. In time of peace, brigades or divisions will not be formed, nor the stations of the troops changed, without authority from the War Department.

ARTICLE IX.

CARE OF FORTIFICATIONS.

40. No person shall be permitted to walk upon any of the slopes of a fortification, excepting the ramps and glacis. If, in any case, it be necessary to provide for crossing them, it should be done by placing wooden steps or stairs against the slopes. The *occasional* walking of persons on a parapet will do no harm, provided it be not allowed to cut the surface into paths.

41. No cattle, horses, sheep, goat, or other animal, shall ever be permitted to go upon the slopes, the ramparts, or the

parapets, nor upon the glacis, except within fenced limits, which should not approach the crest nearer than 30 feet.

43. The burning of grass upon any portion of a fortification is strictly forbidden.

46. The machinery of draw-bridges, gates, and posterns must be kept in good working order by proper cleaning and oiling of the parts; the bridges will be raised, and the gates and posterns opened as often as once a week.

48. The doors and windows of all store-rooms and unoccupied casemates, quarters, barracks, &c., will be opened several times a week for thorough ventilation.

51. No alteration will be made in any fortification, or in its casemates, quarters, barracks, magazines, store-houses, or any other building belonging to it; nor will any building of any kind, or work of earth, masonry, or timber be erected within the fortification, or on its exterior within half a mile, except under the superintendence of the Engineer Department, and by the authority of the Secretary of War.

ARTICLE X.

CARE OF ARMAMENT OF FORTIFICATIONS.

53. All guns should be sponged clean and their vents examined to see that they are clear. The chassis should be traversed and left in a different position, the top carriage moved backward and forward and left alternately over the front and rear transoms of the chassis; the elevating screws or machines wiped clean, worked and oiled if required, and the nuts of all bolts screwed up tight. This should all be done regularly once in every week.

56. The magazine should be frequently examined to see that the powder is well preserved. It should be opened every other day when the air is dry and clear. Barrels of powder should be turned and rolled occasionally. Under ordinary circumstances, only a few cartridges should be kept filled. If the paper body of the cartridge becomes soft or loses its sizing, it is certain that the magazine is

very damp, and some means should be found to improve the ventilation. Cartridge bags may be kept in the magazine ready for filling; also port-fires, fuzes, tubes, and primers. Stands of grape, canisters, and wads for barbette guns, should be kept in store with the implements. For casemate guns, wads may be hung in bundles, and grape and canisters placed near the guns. Shot, well lacquered and clean, may be placed in piles near the guns.

ARTICLE XI.

ARTILLERY PRACTICE.

59. Every commander of a fort or other fixed battery will, before entering on artillery practice, carefully reconnoitre and cause to be sketched for his record-book, the water-channels with their soundings, and other approaches to the work. Buoys, or marks will be placed at the extreme and intermediate ranges of the guns, and these marks be numerically noted on the sketch. A buoy at every five hundred yards may suffice.

60. At the time of practice, a distinct and careful note will be made for the record-book of every shot or shell that may be thrown, designating the guns fired by their numbers, the charges of powder used, the times of flight of shots and shells, the ranges and ricochets, and the positions of guns in respect to the horizontal and vertical lines.

63. On filling from the barrel, the proof range of powder will be marked on the cartridges.

66. Every company with a field battery will be allowed for annual practice as many blank cartridges for the instruction and drill as may be necessary for the purpose, on requisitions duly approved at the proper Departments. Companies with fixed batteries will be allowed 100 cartridges each, with seventy-five shots or shells. This ammunition will be expended in equal parts in the three months designated below, and if the company be mounted, eight blank cartridges will be allowed for each of the other months in the year. This allowance is intended only for compa-

nies *permanently* serving with batteries. The firing with field-guns by other Artillery companies must be confined to *blank* cartridges.

67. For all Artillery there will be annually three periods of practice in firing—*April*, *June*, and *October* for the latitude of Washington and south; and *May*, *July*, and, *September* north of that latitude.

70. As practice in gunnery is a heavy expense to government, commanders of companies and their immediate superiors are charged with the strict execution of the foregoing details; and all officers authorized to make tours of inspection will report, through the prescribed channels, on such execution.

ARTICLE XII.

REGIMENTS.

71. On the organization of a regiment, the companies receive a permanent designation by letters beginning with A, and the officers are assigned to companies; afterward, company officers succeed to companies, as promoted to fill vacancies. Companies take place in the battalion according to the rank of their captains.

72. Captains should be with their companies. Therefore, although subject to the temporary details of service, as for courts-martial, military boards, &c., they shall not, except for urgent reasons, be detailed upon any duty which may separate them for any considerable time from their companies.

73. The commander of a regiment will appoint the adjutant from the subalterns of the regiment. He will nominate the regimental quartermaster to the Secretary of War for appointment if approved. He will appoint the non-commissioned staff of the regiment; and, upon the recommendation of the company commanders, the sergeants and corporals of companies.

74. In cases of vacancy, and till a decision can be had from regimental head-quarters, the company commanders may make temporary appointments of non-commissioned officers.

75. Commanders of regiments are enjoined to avail themselves of every opportunity of instructing both officers and men in the exercise and management of field artillery; and all commanders ought to encourage useful occupations, and manly exercises and diversions among their men, and to repress dissipation and immorality.

76. Regiments serving on foot, being usually employed as light troops, will be habitually exercised in the system of U. S. Tactics for light infantry and riflemen adopted by the War Department, May 1, 1861.

NON-COMMISSIONED OFFICERS.

77. A board, to consist of the Professors of Mathematics and Ethics and the Commandant of Cadets, will convene at the Military Academy, on the first Monday of September in every year, for the examination of such non-commissioned officers, for promotion, as have already passed the regimental examination prescribed in General Orders No. 17, of October 4, 1854.

78. It is enjoined upon all officers to be cautious in reproving non-commissioned officers in the presence or hearing of privates, lest their authority be weakened; and non-commissioned officers are not to be sent to the guard-room and mixed with privates during confinement, but to be considered as placed in arrest, except in aggravated cases, where escape may be apprehended.

79. Non-commissioned officers may be reduced to the ranks by the sentence of a court-martial, or by order of the commander of the regiment on the application of the company commander. If reduced to the rank by garrison courts, at posts not the head-quarters of the regiment, the company commander will immediately forward a transcript of the order to the regimental commander.

80. Every non-commissioned officer shall be furnished with a certificate or warrant of his rank, signed by the colonel and

countersigned by the adjutant. Blank warrants, on parchment, are furnished from the Adjutant-General's office. The first, or orderly sergeant, will be selected by the captain from the sergeants.

81. When it is desired to have bands of music for regiments, there will be allowed for each, sixteen privates to act as musicians, in addition to the chief musicians authorized by law, provided the total number of privates in the regiment, including the band, does not exceed the legal standard. Regimental commanders will without delay designate the proportion to be subtracted from each company for a band, and the "number of recruits required" will be reported accordingly. The companies from which the non-commissioned officers of bands for artillery regiments shall be deducted, will in like manner be designated, and vacancies left accordingly. At the artillery school, Fort Monroe, the non-commissioned officers and privates of the band, will be apportioned among the companies serving at the post.

82. The musicians of the band will, for the time being, be dropped from company muster-rolls, but they will be instructed as soldiers, and liable to serve in the ranks on any occasion. They will be mustered in a separate squad under the chief musician, with the non-commissioned staff, and be included in the aggregate in all regimental returns.

84. No man, unless he be a carpenter, joiner, carriage-maker, blacksmith, saddler, or harness-maker, will be mustered as an "artificer."

85. Every article, excepting arms and accoutrements, belonging to the regiment, is to be marked with the number and name of the regiment.

86. Such articles as belong to companies are to be marked with the letter of the company, and number and name of the regiment; and such as belong to men, with their individual numbers, and the letter of the company.

ARTICLE XIII.

COMPANIES.

90. The captain will cause the men of the company to be numbered, in a regular series, including the non-commissioned officers, and divided into four squads, each to be put under the charge of a non-commissioned officer.

91. Each subaltern officer will be charged with a squad for the supervision of its order and cleanliness; and captains will require their lieutenants to assist them in the performance of *all* company duties.

92. As far as practicable, the men of each squad will be quartered together.

93. The utmost attention will be paid by commanders of companies to the cleanliness of their men, as to their persons, clothing, arms, accoutrements, and equipments, and also as to their quarters or tents.

94. The name of each soldier will be labeled on his bunk, and his company number will be placed against his arms and accoutrements.

95. The arms will be placed in the arm-racks, the stoppers in the muzzles, the cocks let down, and the bayonets in their scabbards; the accoutrements suspended over the arms, and the swords hung up by the belts on pegs.

96. The knapsack of each man will be placed on the lower shelf of his bunk, at its foot, packed with his effects, and ready to be slung; the great-coat on the same shelf, rolled and strapped; the coat, folded inside out, and placed under the knapsack; the cap on the second or upper shelf; and the boots well cleaned.

97. Dirty clothes will be kept in an appropriate part of the knapsack; no article of any kind to be put under the bedding.

98. Cooking utensils and table equipage will be cleaned and arranged in closets or recesses; blacking and brushes out of view; the fuel in boxes.

99. Ordinarily the cleaning will be on Saturdays. The chiefs of squads will cause bunks and bedding to be overhauled; floors dry rubbed; tables and benches scoured; arms cleaned; accoutrements whitened and polished, and every thing put in order.

100. Where conveniences for bathing are to be had, the men should bathe once or twice a week. The feet to be washed at least twice a week. The hair *kept short*, and beard neatly trimmed.

101. Non-commissioned officers, in command of squads, will be held more immediately responsible that their men observe what is prescribed above; that they wash their hands and faces daily; that they brush or comb their heads; that those who are to go on duty put-their arms, accoutrements, dress, &c., in the best order and that such as have permission to pass the chain of sentinels are in the dress that may be ordered.

102. Commanders of companies and squads will see that the arms and accoutrements in possession of the men are always kept in good order, and that proper care be taken in cleaning them.

103. When belts are given to a soldier, the captain will see that they are properly fitted to the body; and it is forbidden to cut any belt without his sanction.

104. Cartridge-boxes and bayonet-scabbards will be polished with blacking; varnish is injurious to the leather, and will not be used.

105. All arms in the hands of the troops, whether browned or bright, will be kept in the state in which they are issued by the Ordnance Department. Arms will not be taken to pieces without permission of a commissioned officer. Bright barrels will be kept clean and free from rust without polishing them; care should be taken in rubbing not to bruise or bend the barrel. After firing, wash out the bore; wipe it dry, and then pass a bit of cloth, slightly greased, to the bottom. In these operations, a rod of wood with a loop in one end is to be used instead of the rammer. The barrel, when not in use, will be closed with a stopper. For exercise, each soldier should keep himself provided with a piece of sole leather to fit the cup or countersink of the hammer.

(For care of arms in service, see Ordnance Manual, page 185, &c.)

106. Arms shall not be left loaded in quarters or tents, or when the men are off duty, except by special orders.

107. Ammunition issued will be inspected frequently. Each man will be made to pay for the rounds expended without orders, or not in the way of duty, or which may be damaged or lost by his neglect.

108. Ammunition will be frequently exposed to the dry air, or sunned.

109. Special care shall be taken to ascertain that no ball-cartridges are mixed with the blank cartridges issued to the men.

110. All knapsacks are to be painted black. Those for the artillery will be marked in the centre of the cover with the number of the regiment only, in figures of one inch and a half in length, of the character called full face, with yellow paint. Those for the infantry will be marked in the same way, in white paint. Those for the ordnance will be marked with two cannon, crossing; the cannon to be seven and a half inches in length, in yellow paint, to resemble those on the cap. The knapsack straps will be black.

111. The knapsacks will also be marked upon the inner side with the letter of the company and the number of the soldier, on such part as may be readily observed at inspections.

112. Haversacks will be marked upon the flap with the number and name of the regiment, the letter of the company, and number of the soldier, in black letters and figures. And each soldier must, at all times, be provided with a haversack and canteen, and will exhibit them at all inspections. It will be worn on the left side on marches, guard, and when paraded for detached service—the canteen outside the haversack.

113. The front of the drums will be painted with the arms of the United States, on a blue field for the infantry, and on a red field for the artillery. The letter of the company and number of the regiment, under the arms, in a scroll.

114. Officers at their stations, in camp or in garrison, will always wear their proper uniform.

115. Soldiers will wear the prescribed uniform in camp or garrison, and will not be permitted to keep in their possession any other clothing. When on fatigue parties, they will wear the proper fatigue dress.

116. In camp or barracks, the company officers must visit the kitchen daily and inspect the kettles, and at all times carefully attend to the messing and economy of their respective companies. The commanding officer of the post or regiment will make frequent inspections of the kitchens and messes. These duties are of the utmost importance—not to be neglected.

117. The bread must be thoroughly baked, and not eaten until it is cold. The soup must be boiled at least five hours, and the vegetables always cooked sufficiently to be perfectly soft and digestible.

118. Messes will be prepared by privates of squads, including private musicians, each taking his tour. The greatest care will be observed in washing and scouring the cooking utensils; those made of brass and copper should be lined with tin.

119. The messes of prisoners will be sent to them by the cooks.

120. No persons will be allowed to visit or remain in the kitchens, except such as may come on duty, or be occupied as cooks. The kitchen should always be under the particular charge of a non-commissioned officer.

121. Those detailed for duty in the kitchens will also be required to keep the furniture of the mess-room in order.

122. On marches and in the field, the only mess furniture of the soldier will be one tin plate, one tin cup, one knife, fork, and spoon, to each man, to be carried by himself on the march.

123. Tradesmen may be relieved from ordinary military duty to make, to alter, or to mend soldiers' clothing, &c. Company commanders will fix the rates at which work shall be done, and cause the men, for whose benefit it is done, to pay for it at the next pay day.

124. Each company officer, serving with his company may take from it one soldier as waiter, with his consent and the con-

sent of his captain. No other officer shall take a soldier as a waiter. Every soldier so employed shall be so reported and mustered.

125. Soldiers taken as officers' waiters shall be acquainted with their military duty, and at all times be completely armed and clothed, and in every respect equipped according to the rules of the service, and have all their necessaries complete and in good order. They are to fall in with their respective companies at all reviews and inspections, and are liable to such drills as the commanding officer shall judge necessary to fit them for service in the ranks.

126. Non-commissioned officers will, in no case, be permitted to act as waiters; nor are they, or private soldiers, not waiters, to be employed in any menial office, or made to perform any service not military, for the private benefit of any officer or mess of officers.

COMPANY BOOKS.

127. The following books are allowed to each company: one descriptive book, one clothing book, one order book, one morning report book, each one quire, sixteen inches by ten. One page of the descriptive book will be appropriated to the list of officers; two to the non-commissioned officers; two to the register of men transferred; four to register of men discharged; two to register of deaths; four to register of deserters—the rest to the company description list.

LAUNDRESS.

128. Four women will be allowed to each company as washerwomen, and will receive one ration per day each.

129. The price of washing soldiers' clothing, by the month, or by the piece, will be determined by the Council of Administration.

130. Debts due the laundress by soldiers, for washing, will be paid, or collected at the pay-table, under the direction of the captain.

ARTICLE XIV.

ORDNANCE SERGEANTS.

131. The Secretary of War selects from the sergeants of the *line* of the army, who may have faithfully served eight years (four years in the grade of non-commissioned officer), as many Ordnance Sergeants as the service may require, not exceeding one to each military post.

132. Captains will report to their colonels such sergeants as, by their conduct and service, merit such appointment, setting forth the description, length of service of the sergeant, the portion of his service he was a non-commissioned officer, his general character as to fidelity and sobriety, his qualifications as a clerk, and his fitness for the duties to be performed by an ordnance sergeant. These reports will be forwarded to the Adjutant-General, to be laid before the Secretary of War, with an application in the following form:

Head-Quarters, &c.

To the Adjutant-General:

SIR:—*I forward, for consideration of the proper authority, an application for the appointment of Ordnance Sergeant.*

Name and Regiment.	Letter of Company.	Length of Service.				Remarks.
		As non-commissioned Officer.		In the Army.		
		Years.	Months.	Years.	Months.	

Inclosed herewith you will receive the report of ——, the officer commanding the company in which the sergeant has been serving, to which I add the following remarks:

————— —————, *Commanding — Regiment.*

134. Ordnance Sergeants will be assigned to posts when appointed, and are not to be transferred to other stations except by orders from the Adjutant-General's office.

137. The appointment and removal of Ordnance Sergeants, stationed at military posts, in pursuance of the above provisions of law, shall be reported by the Adjutant-General to the chief of the Ordnance Department.

138. When a non-commissioned officer receives the appointment of Ordnance Sergeant, he shall be dropped from the rolls of the regiment or company in which he may be serving at the time.

139. The duty of Ordnance Sergeants relates to the care of the ordnance, arms, ammunition, and other military stores at the post to which they may be attached, under the direction of the commanding officer, and according to the regulations of the Ordnance Department.

142. Ordnance Sergeants are to be considered as belonging to the non-commissioned staff of the post, under the orders of the commanding officer. They are to wear the uniform of the Ordnance Department, with the distinctive badges prescribed for the non-commissioned staff of' regiments of artillery; and they are to appear under arms with the troops at all reviews and inspections, monthly and weekly.

ARTICLE XV.

TRANSFER OF SOLDIERS.

145. No non-commissioned officer or soldier will be transferred from one regiment to another without the authority of the commanding general.

146. The colonel may, upon the application of the captains, transfer a non-commissioned officer or soldier from one company to another of his regiment—with consent of the department commander in case of change of post.

ARTICLE XVI.

DECEASED OFFICERS.

149. Whenever an officer dies, or is killed at any military post or station, or in the vicinity of the same, it will be the duty of the commanding officer to report the fact direct to the Adjutant-General, with the date, and any other information proper to be communicated. If an officer die at a distance from a military post, any officer having intelligence of the same will in like manner communicate it, specifying the day of his decease; a duplicate of the report will be sent to Department Head-Quarters.

150. Inventories of the effects of deceased officers, required by the 94th Article of War, will be transmitted to the Adjutant-General.

ARTICLE XVII.

DECEASED SOLDIERS.

152. Inventories of the effects of deceased non-commissioned officers and soldiers, required by the 95th Article of War, will be forwarded to the Adjutant-General, by the commander of the company to which the deceased belonged, and a duplicate of the same to the colonel of the regiment. Final statements of pay, clothing, &c., will be sent with the inventories. When a soldier dies at a post or station absent from his company, it will be the duty of his immediate commander to furnish the required inventory, and, at the same time, to forward to the commanding officer of the company to which the soldier belonged, a report of his death, specifying the date, place, and cause; to what time he was

last paid, and the money or other effects in his possession at the time of his decease; which report will be noted on the next muster-roll of the company to which the man belonged. Each inventory will be indorsed, "Inventory of the effects of ———— ————, late of company (—) ———— regiment of ——, who died at ————, the —— day of ————, 186-." If a legal representative receive the effects, it will be stated in the report. If the soldier leave no effects, the fact will be reported.

ARTICLE XVIII.

DESERTERS.

155. If a soldier desert from, or a deserter be received at, any post other than the station of the company or detachment to which he belonged, he shall be promptly reported by the commanding officer of such post to the commander of his company or detachment. The time of desertion, apprehension, and delivery will be stated. If the man be a recruit, unattached, the required report will be made to the Adjutant-General. When a report is received of the apprehension or surrender of a deserter at any post other than the station of the company or detachment to which he belonged, the commander of such company or detachment shall immediately forward his description and account of clothing to the officer making the report.

156. A reward of five dollars will be paid for the apprehension and delivery of a deserter to an officer of the army at the most convenient post or recruiting station. Rewards thus paid will be promptly reported by the disbursing officer to the officer commanding the company in which the deserter is mustered, and to the authority competent to order his trial. The reward of five dollars will include the remuneration for all expenses incurred for apprehending, securing, and delivering a deserter.

157. When non-commissioned officers or soldiers are sent in pursuit of a deserter, the expenses necessarily incurred will be

paid whether he be apprehended or not, and reported as in case of rewards paid.

158. Deserters shall make good the time lost by desertion, unless discharged by competent authority.

159. No deserter shall be restored to duty without trial, except by authority competent to order the trial.

160. Rewards and expenses paid for apprehending a deserter will be set against his pay, *when adjudged by a court-martial*, or when he is restored to duty without trial on such *condition*.

161. In reckoning the time of service, and the pay and allowances of a deserter, he is to be considered as again in service when delivered up as a deserter to the proper authority.

162. An apprehended deserter, or one who surrenders himself, shall receive no pay while waiting trial, and only such clothing as may be actually necessary for him.

ARTICLE XIX.

DISCHARGES.

163. No enlisted man shall be discharged before the expiration of his term of enlistment without authority of the War Department, except by sentence of a general court-martial, or by the commander of the Department or of an army in the field, on certificate of disability, or on application of the soldier after twenty years' service.

165. Blank discharges on parchment will be furnished from the Adjutant-General's office. No discharge shall be made in duplicate, nor any certificate given in lieu of a discharge.

167. Whenever a non-commissioned officer or soldier shall be unfit for the military service in consequence of wounds, disease, or infirmity, his captain shall forward to the commander of the Department or of the army in the field, through the commander of the regiment or post, a statement of his case, with a certificate of his disability signed by the senior surgeon of the

hospital, regiment, or post, according to the form prescribed in the Medical Regulations.

168. If the recommendation for the discharge of the invalid be approved, the authority therefor will be indorsed on the "certificate of disability," which will be sent back to be completed and signed by the commanding officer, who will then send the same to the Adjutant-General's office.

169. Insane soldiers will not be discharged, but sent, under proper protection, by the Department commander to Washington for the order of the War Department for their admission into the Government Asylum. The history of the cases, with the men's descriptive list, and accounts of pay and clothing, will be sent with them.

ARTICLE XX.

TRAVELING ON DUTY.

173. Whenever an officer traveling under orders arrives at his post, he will submit to the commanding officer a report, in writing, of the time occupied in the travel, with a copy of the orders under which the journey was performed, and an explanation of any delay in the execution of the orders; which report the commanding officer shall transmit, with his opinion on it, to Department Head-Quarters. If the officer be superior in rank to the commander, the required report will be made by the senior himself.

174. Orders detaching an officer for a special duty, imply, unless otherwise stated, that he is thereafter to join his proper station.

ARTICLE XXI.

LEAVES OF ABSENCE TO OFFICERS.

175. In no case will leaves of absence be granted, so that a company be left without one of its *commissioned officers*, or that

a garrisoned post be left without two commissioned officers and competent medical attendance; nor shall leave of absence be granted to an officer during the season of active operations, except on urgent necessity.

177. In time of peace, commanding officers may grant leaves of absence as follows: the commander of a post not to exceed seven days at one time, or in the same month; the commander of a geographical department not to exceed sixty days. Applications for leaves of absence for more than four months, or to officers of engineers, ordnance, or of the general staff, or serving on it (aides-de-camp excepted), for more than thirty days, must be referred to the Adjutant-General for the decision of the Secretary of War. In giving a permission to apply for the extension of a leave of absence, the term of the extension should be stated. The term of the extension approved by the Department commander will be regulated by the season and the usual opportunities for reaching the officer's station, so that he may not be absent during the time for active operations.

183. Officers will not leave the United States, to go beyond sea, without permission from the War Department.

184. All leaves of absence to Chaplains and Schoolmasters employed at military posts will be granted by the commanding officer, on the recommendation of the post Council of Administration, not to exceed four months.

185. An application for leave of absence on account of sickness must be accompanied by a certificate of the senior medical officer present, in the following form:

———— ————, *of the —— regiment of ———, having applied for a certificate on which to ground an application for leave of absence, I do hereby certify that I have carefully examined this officer, and find that —* [Here the nature of the disease, wound, or disability is to be fully stated, and the period during which the officer has suffered under its effects.] *And that, in consequence thereof, he is, in my opinion, unfit for duty. I further declare my belief that he will not be able to resume his duties in a less period than* —— [Here state candidly and explicitly the opinion as to the period which will probably elapse before the officer will be able to resume his duties. When there is no reason to expect a recovery, or when the prospect of recovery is distant and uncertain, or when a change of climate is recommended, it must be so stated.] *Dated at* ——, *this* —— *day of* ——.

Signature of the Medical Officer.

186. Leaves of absence on account of sickness will not be granted to officers to go beyond the limits of the Military Department within which they are stationed, unless the certificate of the medical officer shall explicitly state that a greater change is necessary to save life, or prevent *permanent* disability. Nor will sick leaves to go beyond the Department limits be given in any case, except of immediate urgency, without the previous sanction of the War Department.

189. In all reports of absence, or applications for leave of absence on account of sickness, the officer shall state how long he has been absent already on that account, and by whose permission.

ARTICLE XXII.

FURLOUGHS TO ENLISTED MEN.

190. Furloughs will be granted only by the commanding officer of the post, or the commanding officer of the regiment actually quartered with it. Furloughs may be prohibited at the discretion of the officer in command, and are not to be granted to soldiers about to be discharged.

191. Soldiers on furlough shall not take with them their arms or accoutrements.

192. Form of furlough:

TO ALL WHOM IT MAY CONCERN.

The bearer hereof, ⸺ ⸺, a Sergeant (corporal, or private, as the case may be) of Captain ⸺ ⸺ company, ⸺ regiment of ⸺, aged — years, — feet — inches high, ⸺ complexion, ⸺ eyes, ⸺ hair, and by profession a ⸺; born in the ⸺ of⸺, and enlisted at ⸺, in the ⸺ of ⸺, on the — day of ⸺, eighteen hundred and ⸺, to serve for the period of ⸺, is hereby permitted to go to ⸺, in the county of ⸺, State of ⸺, he having received a Furlough from the — day of ⸺, to the — day of ⸺, at which period he will rejoin his company or regiment at ⸺, or wherever it then may be, or be considered a deserter. Subsistence has been furnished to said ⸺ ⸺ to the — day of ⸺, and pay to the — day of ⸺, both inclusive.

Given under my hand, at ⸺, this — day of ⸺, 18—.

Signature of the officer ⎱ ⸺ ⸺.
giving the furlough. ⎰

ARTICLE XXIII.

COUNCILS OF ADMINISTRATION.

193. The commanding officer of every post shall, at least once in every two months, convene a *Post Council of Administration*, to consist of the *three* regimental or company officers next in rank to himself; or, if there be but two, then the *two* next; if but one, the *one* next; and if there be none other than himself, then he himself shall act.

196. The Post Council shall prescribe the quantity and kind of clothing, small equipments, and soldiers' necessaries, groceries, and all articles which the sutlers may be required to keep on hand; examine the sutler's books and papers, and fix the tariff of prices of the said goods or commodities; inspect the sutler's weights and measures; fix the laundress' charges, and make regulations for the post school.

197. Pursuant to the 30th Article of War, commanding officers reviewing the proceedings of the Council of Administration will scrutinize the tariff of prices proposed by them, and take care that the stores actually furnished by the sutler correspond to the quality prescribed.

POST FUND.

198. A Post Fund shall be raised at each post by a tax on the sutler, not to exceed 10 cents a month for every officer and soldier of the command, according to the average in each month to be ascertained by the Council, and from the saving on the flour ration, ordinarily 33 per cent., by baking the soldiers' bread at a post bakery. Provided, that when want of vegetables or other reasons make it necessary, the commanding officer may order the flour saved, or any part of it, issued to the men, after paying expenses of baking.

200. The following are the objects of expenditure of the post fund:—1st. Expenses of the bake-house; 2d. support of a band; 3d. the post school for soldiers' children; 4th. for formation of a library.

204. The regulations in regard to a post fund will, as far as practicable, be applied in the field to a regimental fund, to be raised, administered, expended, and distributed in like manner, by the regimental commander and a regimental council.

COMPANY FUND.

205. The distributions from the post or regimental fund, and the savings from the company rations, constitute the Company Fund, to be disbursed by the captain for the benefit of the enlisted men of the company, pursuant to resolves of the Company Council, consisting of all the company officers present. In case of a tie vote in the Council, the commander of the post shall decide. The Council shall be convened once in two months by the captain, and whenever else he may think proper.

ARTICLE XXIV.

CHAPLAINS.

208. One chaplain shall be allowed to each regiment of the army, to be appointed by the colonel, on the nomination of the company commanders. None but regularly ordained ministers of some Christian denomination, however, shall be eligible to appointment; and the wishes and wants of the soldiers of the regiment shall be allowed their *full* and *due* weight in making the selection. The proceedings in each case will be immediately forwarded to the Adjutant-General's office, the name and denomination of the chaplain being in every case reported. Chaplains will only be allowed to regiments which are embodied and serving together as one whole—not to regiments of which the companies are serving at different stations.

209. Chaplains, not to exceed thirty in number, are also allowed to posts. The posts at which chaplains may be employed will be announced by the War Department, but the *appointment* will be made by the Council of Administration.

210. The Council of the post will, however, report to the Adjutant-General, for the approval of the Secretary of War, the rate of pay allowed to the person selected to officiate as Chaplain and perform the duties of Schoolmaster; the decision of the Secretary on this point will be notified to the commanding officer of the post by the Adjutant-General.

ARTICLE XXV.

SUTLERS.

211. Every military post may have one Sutler, to be appointed by the Secretary of War.

212. A Sutler shall hold his office for a term of three years, unless sooner removed; but the commanding officer may, for

cause, suspend a Sutler's privilege until a decision of the War Department is received in the case.

214. Troops in campaign, on detachment, or on distant service, will be allowed Sutlers, at the rate of one for every regiment, corps, or separate detachment; to be appointed by the commanding officer of such regiment, corps, or detachment, upon the recommendation of the Council of Administration, subject to the approval of the general or other officer in command.

215. No tax or burden in any shape, other than the authorized assessment for the post fund, will be imposed on the Sutler. If there be a spare building, the use of it may be allowed him, he being responsible that it is kept in repair. If there be no such building, he may be allowed to erect one; but this article gives the Sutler no claim to quarters, transportation for himself or goods, or to any military allowance whatever.

217. No Sutler shall sell to an enlisted man on credit to a sum exceeding *one-third* of his monthly pay, *within the same month*, without the written sanction of the company commander, or the commanding officer of the post or station, if the man does not belong to a company; and not exceeding *one-half* of the monthly pay with such permission.

219. Sutlers shall not farm out or underlet the business and privileges granted by their appointment.

ARTICLE XXVI.

MILITARY DISCUSSIONS AND PUBLICATIONS.

220. Deliberations or discussions among any class of military men, having the object of conveying praise, or censure, or any mark of approbation toward their superiors or others in the military service; and all publications relative to transactions between officers of a private or personal nature, whether newspaper, pamphlet, or hand-bill, are strictly prohibited.

ARTICLE XXVII.

ARRESTS AND CONFINEMENTS.

221. None but commanding officers have power to place officers under arrest except for offenses expressly designated in the 27th Article of War.

222. Officers are not to be put in arrest for light offenses. For these the censure of the commanding officer will, in most cases, answer the purposes of discipline.

223. An officer in arrest may, at the discretion of his commanding officer, have larger limits assigned him than his tent or quarters, on written application to that effect. Close confinement is not to be resorted to unless under circumstances of an aggravated character.

224. In ordinary cases, and where inconvenience to the service would result from it, a medical officer will not be put in arrest until the court-martial for his trial convenes.

225. The arrest of an officer, or confinement of a soldier, will, as soon as practicable, be notified to his immediate commander.

226. All prisoners under guard, without written charges, will be released by the officer of the day at guard-mounting, unless orders to the contrary be given by the commanding officer.

227. On a march, company officers and non-commissioned officers in arrest will follow in the rear of their respective companies, unless otherwise particularly ordered.

228. Field officers, commissioned and non-commissioned staff officers, under the same circumstances, will follow in the rear of their respective regiments.

229. An officer under arrest will not wear a sword, or visit officially his commanding or other superior officer, unless sent for; and in case of business, he will make known his object in writing.

ARTICLE XXVIII.

HOURS OF SERVICE AND ROLL-CALLS.

230. In garrison, *reveille* will be sounded immediately after day-break; and *retreat* at sunset; the *troop, surgeon's call, signals* for breakfast and dinner at the hours prescribed by the commanding officer, according to climate and season. In the cavalry, *stable-calls* immediately after reveille, and an hour and a half before retreat; *water-calls* at the hours directed by the commanding officer.

231. In camp, the commanding officer prescribes the hours of reveille, reports, roll-calls, guard-mounting, meals, stable-calls, issues, fatigues, &c.

232. Signals.

1. To go for fuel—*poing stroke and ten-stroke roll.*
2. To go for water—*two strokes and a flam.*
3. For fatigue party—*pioneer's march.*
4. Adjutant's call—*first part of the troop.*
5. First sergeant's call—*one roll and four taps.*
6. Sergeant's call—*one roll and three taps.*
7. Corporal's call—*one roll and two taps.*
8. For the drummers—*the drummer's call.*

233. The *drummer's call* shall be beat by the drums of the police guard five minutes before the time of beating the stated calls, when the drummers will assemble before the colors of their respective regiments, and as soon as the beat begins on the right, it will be immediately taken up along the line.

ROLL-CALLS.

234. There shall be daily at least three roll-calls, viz., at *reveille, retreat,* and *tattoo.* They will be made on the company parades by the first sergeants, *superintended by a commissioned officer* of the company. The captains will report the absentees without leave to the colonel or commanding officer.

235. Immediately after *reveille* roll-call (after stable-duty in the cavalry), the tents or quarters, and the space around them, will be put in order by the men of the companies, superintended by the chiefs of squads, and the guard-house or guard-tent by the guard or prisoners.

236. The morning reports of companies, signed by the captains and First Sergeants, will be handed to the Adjutant before eight o'clock in the morning, and will be consolidated by the Adjutant within the next hour, for the information of the Colonel; and if the consolidation is to be sent to higher authority, it will be signed by the Colonel and the Adjutant.

ARTICLE XXIX.

HONORS TO BE PAID BY THE TROOPS.

237. The *President* or *Vice-President* is to be saluted with the highest honors—all standards and colors dropping, officers and troops saluting. drums beating and trumpets sounding.

238. *A General commanding-in-chief* is to be received—by cavalry, with sabres presented, trumpets sounding the march, and all the officers saluting, standards dropping; by infantry, with drums beating the march, colors dropping, officers saluting, and arms presented.

239. *A Major-General* is to be received—by cavalry, with sabres presented, trumpets sounding twice the trumpet-flourish, and officers saluting; by infantry, with three ruffles, colors dropping, officers saluting, and arms presented.

240. *A Brigadier-General* is to be received—by cavalry, with sabres presented, trumpets sounding once the trumpet-flourish, and officers saluting; by infantry, with two ruffles, colors dropping, officers saluting, and arms presented.

241. *An Adjutant-General* or *Inspector-General*, if under the rank of a General officer, is to be received at a review or inspection of the troops under arms—by cavalry, with sabres presented, officers saluting; by infantry, officers saluting and arms presented.

The same honors to be paid to any field-officer authorized to review and inspect the troops. When the inspecting officer is junior to the officer commanding the parade, no compliments will be paid: he will be received only with swords drawn and arms shouldered.

242. All guards are to turn out and present arms to *General officers* as often as they pass them, except the personal guards of General officers, which turn out only to the Generals whose guards they are, and to officers of superior rank.

243. To commanders of regiments, garrison, or camp, their own guard turn out, and present arms once a day; after which, they turn out with shouldered arms.

244. *To the members of the Cabinet; to the Chief Justice, the President of the Senate, and Speaker of the House of Representatives of the United States; and to Governors, within their respective States and Territories*—the same honors will be paid as to a General commanding-in-chief.

245. *Officers of a foreign service* may be complimented with the honors due to their rank.

246. *American and Foreign Envoys or Ministers* will be received with the compliments due to a Major-General.

247. The colors of a regiment passing a guard are to be saluted, the trumpets sounding, and the drums beating a march.

248. When General officers, or persons entitled to salute, pass in the rear of a guard, the officer is only to make his men stand shouldered, and not to face his guard about, or beat his drum.

249. When General officers, or persons entitled to a salute, pass guards while in the act of relieving, both guards are to salute, receiving the word of command from the senior officer of the whole.

250. All guards are to be under arms when armed parties approach their posts; and to parties commanded by commissioned officers, they are to present their arms, drums beating a march, and officers saluting.

251. No compliments by guards or sentinels will be paid between *retreat* and *reveille*, except as prescribed for *grand rounds*.

252. All guards and sentinels are to pay the same compliments to the officers of the navy, marines, and militia, in the service of the United States, as are directed to be paid to the officers of the army, according to their relative ranks.

253. It is equally the duty of non-commissioned officers and soldiers, *at all times* and *in all situations*, to pay the proper compliments to officers of the navy and marines, and to officers of other regiments, when in uniform, as to officers of their own particular regiments and corps.

254. Courtesy among military men is indispensable to discipline. Respect to superiors will not be confined to obedience on duty, but will be extended to all occasions. It is always the duty of the inferior to accost or to offer first the customary salutation, and of the superior to return such complimentary notice.

255. Sergeants, with swords drawn, will salute by bringing them to a present—with muskets, by bringing the left hand across the body, so as to strike the musket near the right shoulder. Corporals out of the ranks, and privates not sentries, will carry their muskets at a shoulder as sergeants, and salute in like manner.

256. When a soldier without arms, or with side-arms only, meets an officer, he is to raise his hand to the right side of the visor of his cap, palm to the front, elbow raised as high as the shoulder, looking at the same time in a respectful and soldier-like manner at the officer, who will return the compliment thus offered.

257. A non-commissioned officer or soldier being seated, and without particular occupation, will rise on the approach of an officer, and make the customary salutation. If standing, he will turn toward the officer for the same purpose. If the parties remain in the same place or on the same ground, such compliments need not be repeated.

SALUTES.

258. The national salute is determined by the number of States composing the Union, at the rate of one gun for each State.

259. The *President of the United States* alone is to receive a salute of twenty-one guns.

260. The *Vice-President* is to receive a salute of seventeen guns.

261. The *Heads of the great Executive Departments of the National Government;* the *General commanding the army;* the *Governors of States and Territories*, within their respective jurisdictions, fifteen guns.

262. A *Major-General*, thirteen guns.

263. A *Brigadier-General*, eleven guns.

264. *Foreign ships of war* will be saluted in return for a similar compliment, gun for gun, on notice being officially received of such intention. If there be several posts in sight of, or within six miles of each other, the principal only shall reciprocate compliments with ships passing.

265. *Officers of the Navy* will be saluted according to relative rank.

266. *Foreign Officers* invited to visit a fort or post may be saluted according to their relative rank.

267. *Envoys and Ministers* of the United States and foreign powers are to be saluted with thirteen guns.

268. A General officer will be saluted but once in a year at each visit and only when notice of his intention to visit the post has been given.

269. Salutes to individuals are to be fired on their arrival only.

270. A national salute will be fired at meridian on the anniversary of the Independence of the United States, at each military post and camp provided with artillery and ammunition.

ESCORTS OF HONOR.

271. Escorts of honor may be composed of cavalry or infantry, or both, according to circumstances. They are guards of honor for the purpose of receiving and escorting personages of

high rank, civil or military. The troops for this purpose will be selected for their soldierly appearance and superior discipline.

FUNERAL HONORS.

275. On the receipt of official intelligence of the death of the *President of the United States*, at any post or camp, the commanding officer shall, on the following day, cause a gun to be fired at every half hour, beginning at sunrise, and ending at sunset. When posts are contiguous, the firing will take place only at the post commanded by the superior officer.

276. On the day of the interment of a *General commanding-in-chief*, a gun will be fired at every half hour, until the procession moves, beginning at sunrise.

277. The funeral escort of a *General commanding-in-chief* shall consist of a regiment of infantry, a squadron of cavalry, and six pieces of artillery.

278. That of a *Major-General*, a regiment of infantry, a squadron of cavalry, and four pieces of artillery.

279. That of a *Brigadier-General*, a regiment of infantry, one company of cavalry, and two pieces of artillery.

280. That of a *Colonel*, a regiment.

281. That of a *Lieutenant-Colonel*, six companies.

282. That of a *Major*, four companies.

283. That of a *Captain*, one company.

284. That of a *Subaltern*, half a company.

285. The funeral escort shall always be commanded by an officer of the same rank with the deceased; or, if none such be present, by one of the next inferior grade.

286. The funeral escort of a non-commissioned staff officer shall consist of sixteen rank and file, commanded by a Sergeant.

287. That of a Sergeant, of fourteen rank and file, commanded by a Sergeant.

288. That of a Corporal, of twelve rank and file, commanded by a Corporal; and,

289. That of a private, of eight rank and file, commanded by a Corporal.

290. The escort will be formed in two ranks, opposite to the quarters or tent of the deceased, with shouldered arms and bayonets unfixed; the artillery and cavalry on the right of the infantry.

299. The usual badge of military mourning is a piece of black crape around the left arm, above the elbow, and also upon the sword-hilt; and will be worn when in full or in undress.

300. As family mourning, crape will be worn by officers (when in uniform) only around the left arm.

301. The drums of a funeral escort will be covered with black crape, or thin black serge.

ARTICLE XXX.

INSPECTIONS OF THE TROOPS.

303. The inspection of troops, as a division, regiment, or other body composing a garrison or command, not less than a company, will generally be preceded by a review.

304. There will be certain periodical inspections, to wit:

1. The commanders of regiments and posts will make an inspection of their commands on the last day of every month.
2. Captains will inspect their companies every Sunday morning. No soldier will be excused from Sunday inspection except the guard, the sick, and the necessary attendants in the hospital.
3. Medical officers having charge of hospitals will also make a thorough inspection of them every Sunday morning.
4. Inspection when troops are mustered for payment.

305. Besides these inspections, frequent visits will be made by the commanding officer, company and medical officers, during the month, to the men's quarters, the hospital, guard-house, &c.

FORM OF INSPECTION.

306. The present example embraces a battalion of infantry. The inspecting officer and the field and staff officers will be on foot.

307. The battalion being in the order of battle, the Colonel will cause it to break into open column of companies, right in front. He will next order the ranks to be opened, when the color-rank and color-guard, under the direction of the Adjutant, will take post ten paces in front, and the band two paces in rear of the column.

320. The inspection of the troops being ended, the field and staff will next accompany the Inspector to the hospital, magazine, arsenal, quarters, sutler's shop, guard-house, and such other places as he may think proper to inspect. The Captains and subalterns repair to their companies and sections to await the Inspector.

321. The hospital being at all times an object of particular interest, it will be critically and minutely inspected.

324. The Adjutant will exhibit to the Inspector the regimental books and papers, including those relating to the transactions of the Council of Administration. The company books and papers will also be exhibited, the whole together, generally at the Adjutant's office, and in the presence of the officers not otherwise particularly engaged.

325. The Inspector will examine critically the books and accounts of the administrative and disbursing officers of the command, and the money and property in their keeping.

326. The inspection of cavalry and artillery will conform to the principles laid down in the foregoing paragraphs, regard being had to the system of instruction for those arms of service respectively.

ARTICLE XXXI.

MUSTERS.

327. Troops will be mustered for pay on the last day of February, April, June, August, October, and December. The musters will be made by an Inspector-General, if present, otherwise by an officer specially designated by the Commander of the Army, Division, or Department; and in absence of either an Inspector-General or officer specially designated, the muster will be made by the commander of the post.

329. All stated musters of the troops shall be preceded by a minute and careful *inspection* in the prescribed mode; and if the command be of more than a company, by a *review*, before inspection.

330. The mustering officer will then call over the names on the roll, and each man, as his name is called, will distinctly answer, *Here!* and bring his piece to a *carry* and to an *order*.

332. After mustering the companies, the mustering officer, attended by the company commanders, will visit the guard and hospital, to verify the presence of the men reported there.

ARTICLE XXXII.

FORMS OF PARADE.

I. DRESS PARADE

337. There shall be daily one dress parade, at *troop* or *retreat*, as the commanding officer may direct.

338. A signal will be beat or sounded half an hour before *troop* or *retreat*, for the music to assemble on the regimental parade, and each company to turn out under arms on its own parade, for roll-call and inspection by its own officers.

347. All field and company officers and men will be present at *dress parades*, unless especially excused, or on some duty incompatible with such attendance.

348. A dress parade once a day will not be dispensed with, except on extraordinary and urgent occasions.

374. The review of Cavalry and Artillery will be conducted on similar principles, and according to the systems of instruction for those Arms of Service.

III. GUARD-MOUNTING.

375. Camp and garrison guards will be relieved every twenty-four hours. The guards at outposts will ordinarily be relieved in the same manner, but this must depend on their distances from camp, or other circumstances, which may sometimes require their continuing on duty several days. In such cases, they must be previously warned to provide themselves accordingly.

376. At the first call for guard-mounting, the men warned for duty turn out on their company parades for inspection by the First Sergeants; and at the second call, repair to the regimental or garrison parade, conducted by the First Sergeants. Each detachment, as it arrives, will, under the direction of the Adjutant, take post on the left of the one that preceded it, in open order, arms shouldered, and bayonets fixed; the supernumeraries five paces in the rear of the men of their respective companies; the First Sergeants in rear of them. The Sergeant-Major will dress the ranks, count the files, verify the details, and when the guard is formed, report to the Adjutant, and take post two paces on the left of the front rank.

377. The Adjutant then commands *Front*, when the officer of the guard takes post twelve paces in front of the centre, the Sergeants in one rank, four paces in the rear of the officers; and the Corporals in one rank, four paces in the rear of the Sergeants—all facing to the front. The Adjutant then assigns their places in the guard.

ARTICLE XXXIII.

GUARDS.

399. Sentinels will be relieved every two hours, unless the state of the weather, or other causes, should make it necessary or proper that it be done at shorter or longer intervals.

400. Each relief, before mounting, is inspected by the commander of the guard or of its post. The Corporal reports to him, and presents the old relief on its return.

401. The *countersign*, or watchword, is given to such persons as are entitled to pass during the night, and to officers, non-commissioned officers, and sentinels of the guard. Interior guards receive the countersign only when ordered by the commander of the troops.

404. The officer of the day must see that the officer of the guard is furnished with the parole and countersign before *retreat*.

410. The officer of the guard must see that the countersign is duly communicated to the sentinels a little before twilight.

413. Sentinels will not take orders or allow themselves to be relieved, except by an officer or non-commissioned officer of their guard or party, the officer of the day, or the commanding officer; in which case the orders will be immediately notified to the commander of the guard by the officer giving them.

414. Sentinels will report every breach of orders or regulations they are instructed to enforce.

415. Sentinels must keep themselves on the alert, observing every thing that takes place within sight and hearing of their post. They will carry their arms habitually at support, or on either shoulder, but will never quit them. In wet weather, if there be no sentry-box, they will secure arms.

416. No sentinel shall quit his post or hold conversation not necessary to the proper discharge of his duty.

417. All persons, of whatever rank in the service, are required to observe respect toward sentinels.

418. In case of disorder, a sentinel must call out *the guard*; and if a fire take place, he must cry; *"Fire!"* adding the number of his post. If in either case the danger be great, he must discharge his firelock before calling out.

419. It is the duty of a sentinel to repeat all calls made from posts more distant from the main body of the guard than his own, and no sentinel will be posted so distant as not to be heard by the guard, either directly or through other sentinels.

427. When any person approaches a post of the guard at night, the sentinel before the post, after challenging, causes him to halt until examined by a non-commissioned officer of the guard.

428. The officer of the day, wishing to make the rounds, will take an escort of a non-commissioned officer and two men.

ARTICLE XXXIV.

ORDERS AND CORRESPONDENCE.

432. The orders of commanders of armies, divisions, brigades, regiments, are denominated orders of such army, division, &c., and are either general or special. Orders are numbered, general and special, in separate series, each beginning with the year.

433. General orders announce the time and place of issues and payments; hours for roll-calls and duties; the number and kind of orderlies, and the time when they shall be relieved; police regulations, and the prohibitions required by circumstances and localities; returns to be made, and their forms; laws and regulations for the army; promotions and appointments; eulogies or censures to corps or individuals, and generally, whatever it may be important to make known to the whole command.

434. Special orders are such as do not concern the troops generally, and need not be published to the whole command; such as relate to the march of some particular corps, the establishment of some post, the detaching of individuals, the granting requests, &c., &c.

435. A general order, and an important special order, must be read and approved by the officer whose order it is, before it is issued by the staff officer.

438. Orders are transmitted through all the intermediate commanders in the order of rank. When an intermediate commander is omitted, the officer who gives the order shall inform him, and he who receives it shall report it to his immediate superior.

439. Orders for any body of troops will be addressed to the commander, and will be opened and executed by the commander present, and published or distributed by him when necessary; printed orders, however, are generally distributed direct to posts from the head-quarters where issued.

442. If general orders are not received in regular succession, commanding officers will report the missing numbers to the proper headquarters.

443. The orderly hours being fixed at each head-quarters, the staff officers and chiefs of the special services either attend in person, or send their assistants to obtain the orders of the day; and the first sergeants of companies repair for that purpose to the regimental or garrison headquarters.

444. During marches and active operations, and when the regular orderly hours cannot be observed, all orders will be either sent direct to the troops, or the respective commanders of regiments or corps will be informed when to send to head-quarters for them. Under the same circumstances, orders will be read to the troops during a halt, without waiting for the regular parades.

456. Letters on letter paper will be folded in three folds, parallel with the writing.

457. All communications on public service are to be marked on the cover, "*Official Business.*"

ARTICLE XXXV.

RETURNS AND REPORTS.

MONTHLY RETURNS.

458. Commanders of regiments, corps, and posts, will make to the Adjutant-General's office of the War Department monthly returns of their respective regiments, corps, and posts, on the forms furnished from that office, and according to the directions expressed on them. In like manner, Captains make monthly company returns to regimental headquarters. All monthly returns will be forwarded on the 1st day of the next month, except regimental returns, which are forwarded as soon as all the company returns are received.

ANNUAL RETURNS—CASUALTIES.

462. This return will exhibit the various changes and alterations which may have taken place in the regiment during the preceding twelve months: that is to say, a statement of the number of resignations, transfers, deaths, &c., of commissioned officers; the number of men joined by enlistment, transferred, and discharged; the number tried by Courts-Martial or by the civil law, and the nature of their offenses; the number of discharges, deaths, dismissals, and desertions; number joined from desertion, pardoned, &c., &c.

RETURN OF DECEASED SOLDIERS.

463. To be forwarded to the Adjutant-General, by the Colonels of regiments, *quarterly*. Also a duplicate to the Second Auditor of the Treasury.

FIELD RETURNS.

464. Besides the stated returns of the troops, such other *field returns* and reports will be made as may be necessary to keep the government informed of the condition and strength of the forces.

465. After any action or affair, a return of the killed, wounded, and missing will be made, in which the name, rank, and regiment of each officer and soldier will be specified, with such remarks and explanations as may be requisite for the records of the Department of War, or be necessary to establish the just claims of any individual who may have been wounded, or of the heirs and representatives of any killed in action (taking care to specify the *nature of the wound*, the *time* and *place* of its occurrence, the company, regiment, or corps, and the name of the Captain, Colonel, or other commanding officer).

REPORTS.

466. The date of appointment, of detail, and of removal of all staff officers, or of officers selected for duty in staff departments, which may entitle them to receive additional pay, will be immediately reported by the officer making such appointment, detail, or removal, to the Adjutant-General, and to the Paymaster of the department or command to which such officers belong.

PRISONERS OF WAR—CAPTURED PROPERTY.

469. A return of prisoners, and a report of the number and description of the killed and wounded of the enemy, will be forwarded to the Adjutant-General's office, Washington.

470. A return of all property captured will be made by the commanding officer of the troops by whom such capture was made, to the Adjutant-General, at Washington, in order that it may be disposed of according to the orders of the War Department.

INSPECTION REPORTS.

471. Inspection reports will show the discipline of the troops; their instruction in all military exercises and duties: the state of their arms, clothing, equipments, and accoutrements of all kinds; of their kitchens and messes; of the barracks and quar-

ters at the post; of the guardhouse, prisons, hospital, bake-house, magazines, store-houses, and stores of every description; of the stables and horses; the condition of the post school; the management and application of the post and company funds; the state of the post, and regimental, and company books, papers, and files; the zeal and ability of the officers in command of troops; the capacity of the officers conducting the administrative and staff services, the fidelity and economy of their disbursements; the condition of all public property, and the amount of money in the hands of each disbursing officer; the regularity of issues and payments; the mode of enforcing discipline by courts-martial, and by the authority of the officers; the propriety and legality of all punishments inflicted; and any information whatsoever concerning the service, in any matter or particular that may merit notice, or aid to correct defects or introduce improvements.

472. Inspectors are required particularly to report if any officer is of intemperate habits, or unfit for active service by infirmity or any other cause.

ARTICLE XXXVI.

TROOPS IN CAMPAIGN.

ORGANIZATION OF AN ARMY IN THE FIELD.

473. The formation by divisions is the basis of the organization and administration of armies in the field.

474. A division consists usually of two or three brigades, either of infantry or cavalry, and troops of other corps in the necessary proportion.

475. A brigade is formed of two or more regiments. The first number takes the right.

476. Mixed brigades are sometimes formed of infantry and light cavalry, especially for the advanced guards.

477. As the troops arrive at the rendezvous, the general commanding-in-chief will organize them into brigades and divisions.

478. The light cavalry is employed as flankers and partisans, and generally for all service out of the line.

479. Heavy cavalry belongs to the reserve, and is covered, when necessary, in marches, camps, or bivouacs, by light troops, or infantry of the line.

480. The arrangement of the troops on parade and in order of battle is—1st, the light infantry; 2d, infantry of the line; 3d, light cavalry; 4th, cavalry of the line; 5th, heavy cavalry. The troops of the artillery and engineers are in the centre of the brigades, divisions, or corps to which they are attached; marines take the left of other infantry; volunteers and militia take the left of regular troops of the same arm, and among themselves, regiments of volunteers or militia of the same arm take place by lot. This arrangement is varied by the general commanding-in-chief, as the circumstances of war render expedient.

481. Brigades in divisions, and divisions in the army, are numbered from right to left; but in reports of military operations, brigades and divisions are designated by the name of the general commanding them.

482. The order of regiments in brigades and of brigades in divisions may be changed by the commander of the division for important reasons, such as the weakness of some corps, or to relieve one from marching too long at the rear of the column. Such changes must be reported to the general commanding-in-chief.

483. The general commanding-in-chief assigns the generals of divisions and of brigades to their respective commands, when the assignment is not made by the Department of War.

CONTRIBUTIONS.

491. When the wants of the army absolutely require it, and in other cases, under special instructions from the War Department, the general commanding the army may levy contributions in money or kind on the enemy's country occupied by the troops.

No other commander can levy such contributions without written authority from the general commanding-in-chief.

ORDERLIES.

492. At the opening of a campaign, the commander of an army determines and announces in orders the number of orderlies, mounted or foot, for the Generals, and the corps or regiments by which they are to be supplied, and the periods at which they shall be relieved.

493. In marches, the mounted orderlies follow the Generals, and perform the duty of escorts, or march with orderlies on foot at the head of the division or brigade.

495. Mounted soldiers are to be employed to carry dispatches only in special and urgent cases. (See par. 557.)

DEPÔTS.

497. The grand depôts of an army are established where the military operations would not expose them to be broken up. Smaller depôts are organized for the divisions and the several arms. They are commanded by officers temporarily disabled for field service, or by other officers when necessary, and comprise, as much as possible, the hospitals and depôts for convalescents. When conveniently placed, they serve as points for the halting and assembling of detachments. They receive the disabled from the corps on the march; and the officers in command of the depôts send with the detachments to the army those at the depôts who have become fit for service.

CAMPS.

498. A camp is the place where troops are established in tents, in huts, or in bivouac. Cantonments are the inhabited places which troops occupy for shelter when not put in barracks. The camping-party is a detachment detailed to prepare a camp.

Plate 1.

Camp of a Regiment of Infantry.

Cl.—*Colonel.*
Lt. Cl.—*Lieut. Colonel.*
M.—*Major.*
Surg.—*Surgeon.*

Ast. Surg.—*Asst. Surgeon.*
Adjt.—*Adjutant.*
Q. M.—*Quarter Master.*
n-c-s.—*Non.-Com.-Staff.*

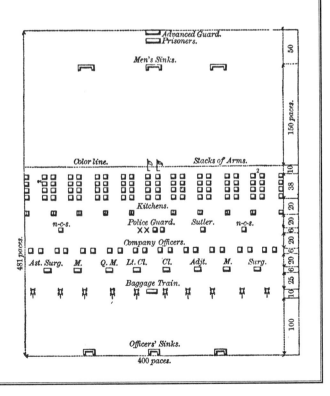

Advanced Guard.
Prisoners.

50

Men's Sinks.

150 paces.

10

Color line. *Stacks of Arms.*

38

Kitchens.

20

n-c-s. *Police Guard.* *Sutler.* *n-c-s.*

6 20

Company Officers.

6 20

Ast. Surg. *M.* *Q. M.* *Lt. Cl.* *Cl.* *Adjt.* *M.* *Surg.*

6 20

481 paces.

Baggage Train.

25 10

100

Officers' Sinks.

400 paces.

500. The camping-party of a regiment consists of the regimental Quartermaster and Quartermaster-Sergeant, and a Corporal and two men per company. The General decides whether the regiments camp separately or together, and whether the police guard shall accompany the camping-party, or a larger escort shall be sent.

501. Neither baggage nor led horses are permitted to move with the camping-party.

513. No officer will be allowed to occupy a house, although vacant and on the ground of his camp, except by permission of the commander of the brigade, who shall report it to the commander of the division.

CAMP OF INFANTRY.

515. Each company has its tents in two files, facing on a street perpendicular to the color line. The width of the street depends on the front of the camp, but should not be less than 5 paces. The interval between the ranks of tents is 2 paces; between the files of tents of adjacent companies, 2 paces; between regiments, 22 paces.

CAMP OF CAVALRY.

524. In the cavalry, each company has one file of tents—the tents opening on the street facing the left of the camp.

525. The horses of each company are placed in a single file, facing the opening of the tents, and are fastened to pickets planted firmly in the ground, from 3 to 6 paces from the tents of the troops.

526. The interval between the file of tents should be such that, the regiment being broken into column of companies [as indicated in plate], each company should be on the extension of the line on which the horses are to be picketed.

535. The field and staff have their horses on the left of their tents, on the same line with the company horses; sick horses are

Camp of a Regiment of Five Squadrons of Cavalry.

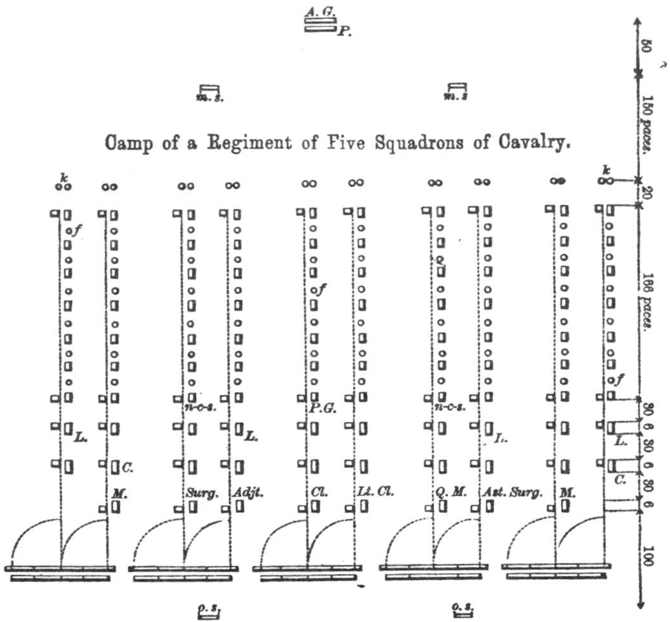

Plate 2.

Cl.—Colonel.
Lt. Cl.—Lieut. Colonel.
M.—Major.
Surg.—Surgeon.
Ast. Surg.—Asst. Surgeon.
Adjt.—Adjutant.
Q. M.—Quartermaster.
C.—Captain.
L.—Lieutenant.
A. G.—Advanced Guard.
P. G.—Police Guard.
m. s.—Men's Sinks.
o. s.—Officers' sinks.
k.—Kitchens.
f.—Forage.
n-c-s.—Non-Com-Staff.
P.—Prisoners.

placed in one line on the right or left of the camp. The men who attend them have a separate file of tents; the forges and wagons in rear of this file. The horses of the train and of camp-followers are in one or more files extending to the rear, behind the right or left squadron. The advanced post of the police guard is 200 paces in front, opposite the centre of the regiment; the horses in one or two files.

CAMP OF ARTILLERY.

537. The artillery is encamped near the troops to which it is attached, so as to be protected from attack, and to contribute to the defense of the camp. Sentinels for the park are furnished by the artillery, and, when necessary, by the other troops.

BIVOUACS.

540. A regiment of cavalry being in order of battle, in rear of the ground to be occupied, the Colonel breaks it by platoons to the right. The horses of each platoon are placed in a single row, and fastened as prescribed for camps; near the enemy, they remain saddled all night, with slackened girths. The arms are at first stacked in rear of each row of horses; the sabres, with the bridles hung on them, are placed against the stacks.

541. The forage is placed on the right of each row of horses. Two stable-guards for each platoon watch the horses.

CANTONMENTS.

548. The cavalry should be placed under shelter whenever the distance from the enemy, and from the ground where the troops are to form for battle, permit it. Taverns and farm-houses, with large stables and free access, are selected for quartering them.

552. When cavalry and infantry canton together, the latter furnish the guards by night, and the former by day.

553. Troops cantoned in presence of the enemy should be covered by advanced guards and by natural or artificial obstacles. Cantonments taken during a cessation of hostilities should be

established in rear of a line of defense, and in front of the point on which the troops would concentrate to receive an attack. The General commanding-in-chief assigns the limits of their cantonments to the divisions, the commanders of divisions to brigades, and the commanders of brigades post their regiments. The position for each corps in case of attack is carefully pointed out by the Generals.

HEAD-QUARTERS.

554. Generals take post at the centre of their commands, on the main channels of communication. If troops bivouac in presence of the enemy, the Generals bivouac with them.

MILITARY EXERCISES.

555. When troops remain in camp or cantonment many days, the Colonels require them to be exercised in the school of the battalion and squadron. Regiments and brigades encamped by division are not united for drills without the permission of the General of division. The troops must not be exercised at the firings without the authority of the General commanding-in-chief. The practice of the drums must never begin with the " general," or the "march of the regiment;" nor the trumpets with the sound "to horse." The hour for practice is always announced.

ORDERS.

556. In the field, verbal orders and important sealed orders are carried by officers, and, if possible, by staff officers. When orders are carried by orderlies, the place and time of departure will be marked on them, and place and time of delivery on the receipt.

DISPATCHES.

557. Dispatches, particularly for distant corps, should be intrusted only to officers to whom their contents can be confided. In a country occupied by the enemy, the bearer of dispatches

should be accompanied by at least two of the best mounted men; should avoid towns and villages, and the main roads; rest as little as possible, and only at out-of-the-way places. Where there is danger, he should send one of the men in advance, and be always ready to destroy his dispatches. He should be adroit in answering questions about the army, and not to be intimidated by threats.

WATCHWORDS.

558. The parole and countersign are issued daily from the principal head-quarters of the command. The countersign is given to the sentinels and non-commissioned officers of guards; the parole to the commissioned officers of guards. The parole is usually the name of a general, the countersign that of a battle.

559. When the parole and countersign cannot be communicated daily to a post or detachment which ought to use the same as the main body, a series of words may be sent for some days in advance.

560. If the countersign is lost, or one of the guard deserts with it, the commander on the spot will substitute another, and report the case at once to the proper superior, that immediate notice may be given to head-quarters.

ISSUES.

561. At what time and for what period issues are made, must depend on circumstances, and be regulated in orders. When an army is not moving, rations are generally issued for four days at a time. Issues to the companies of a regiment, and the fatigues to receive them, are superintended by an officer detailed from the regiment. Issues are made from one end of the line to the other, beginning on the right and left, alternately. An issue commenced to one regiment will not be interrupted for another entitled to precedence if it had been in place.

THE ROSTER, OR DETAILS FOR SERVICE.

562. The duties performed by detail are of three classes. The *first class* comprises, 1st. grand guards and outposts; 2d. interior guards, as of magazine, hospital, &c.; 3d. orderlies; 4th. police guards.

The *second class* comprises, 1st. detachments to protect laborers on military works, as field works, communications, &c.; 2d. working parties on such works; 3d. detachments to protect fatigues.

The *third class* are all fatigues, without arms, in or out of camp.

In the cavalry, stable-guards form a separate roster, and count before fatigue.

565. Officers, non-commissioned officers, and soldiers take duties of the first class in the order stated, viz., the first, for the detail, takes the grand guards; the next, the interior guards; the last, the police guard; and the same rule in regard to the details and duties of the second class. In the details for the third class, the senior officer takes the largest party. The party first for detail takes the service out of camp.

566. When the officer whose tour it is, is not able to take it, or is not present at the hour of marching, the next after him takes it. When a guard has passed the chain of sentinels, or an interior guard has reached its post, the officer whose tour it was cannot then take it. He takes the tour of the officer who has taken his. When an officer is prevented by sickness from taking his tour, it passes. These rules apply equally to non-commissioned officers and soldiers.

569. Soldiers march with knapsacks on all duties of the first class; and with arms and equipments complete on all working parties out of the camp, unless otherwise ordered. In the cavalry, horses are packed for all mounted service.

570. In the cavalry, dismounted men, and those who horses are not in order, are preferred for the detail for dismounted

service. Those who are mounted are never employed on those services, if the number of the other class are sufficient.

571. Every non-commissioned officer and soldier in the cavalry detailed for dismounted service must, before he marches, take to the First Sergeant of the troop, or Sergeant of his squad, his horse equipments and his valise ready packed. In case of alarm, the First Sergeant sees that the horses of these men are equipped and led to the rendezvous.

POLICE GUARD.

573. In each regiment a police guard is detailed every day, consisting of two sergeants, three corporals, two drummers, and men enough to furnish the required sentinels and patrols. The men are taken from all the companies, from each in proportion to its strength. The guard is commanded by a Lieutenant, under the supervision of a Captain, as regimental officer of the day. It furnishes ten sentinels at the camp: one over the arms of the guard; one at the Colonel's tent; three on the color front, one of them over the colors; three, fifty paces in rear of the field officers' tents; and one on each flank, between it and the next regiment. If it is a flank regiment, one more sentinel is posted on the outer flank.

574. An advanced post is detached from the police guard, composed of a sergeant, a corporal, a drummer, and nine men to furnish sentinels and the guard over the prisoners. The men are the first of the guard roster from each company. The men of the advanced post must not leave it under any pretext. Their meals are sent to the post. The advanced post furnishes three sentinels; two a few paces in front of the post, opposite the right and left wing of the regiment, posted so as to see as far as possible to the front, and one over the arms.

575. In the cavalry, dismounted men are employed in preference on the police guard. The mounted men on guard are sent in succession, a part at a time, to groom their horses. The advanced post is always formed of mounted men.

576. In each company, a corporal has charge of the stable-guard. His tour begins at retreat, and ends at morning stable-call. The stable-guard is large enough to relieve the men on post every two hours. They sleep in their tents, and are called by the corporal when wanted. At retreat he closes the streets of the camp with cords, or uses other precautions to prevent the escape of loose horses.

577. The officer of the day is charged with the order and cleanliness of the camp: a fatigue is furnished to him when the number of prisoners is insufficient to clean the camp. He has the calls beaten by the drummer of the guard.

582. The sentinels on the front of the advanced post have orders to permit neither non-commissioned officers nor soldiers to pass the line, without reporting at the advanced post; to warn the advanced post of the approach of any armed body, and to arrest all suspicious persons. The sergeant sends persons so arrested to the officer of the guard, and warns him of the approach of any armed body.

583. The sentinel over the arms at the advanced post guards the prisoners and keeps sight of them, and suffers no one to converse with them without permission. They are only permitted to go to the sinks one at a time, and under a sentinel.

584. If any one is to be passed out of camp at night, the officer of the guard sends him under escort to the advanced post, and the sergeant of the post has him passed over the chain.

586. The officer of the day satisfies himself frequently during the night, of the vigilance of the police guard and advanced post. He prescribes patrols and rounds to be made by the officer and non-commissioned officers of the guard. The officer of the guard orders them when he thinks necessary. He visits the sentinels frequently.

THE PICKET.

593. The detail for the picket is made daily, after the details for duty of the first class, and from the next for detail on the

roster of that class. It is designed to furnish detachments and guards unexpectedly called for in the twenty-four hours; it counts as a tour of the first class to those who have marched on detachment or guard, or who have passed the night in bivouac.

594. The officers, non-commissioned officers, and soldiers of the picket are at all times dressed and equipped; the horses are saddled, and knapsacks and valises ready to be put on.

597. The picket is assembled by the Adjutant at guard-mounting; it is posted twelve paces in rear of the guard, and is inspected by its own commander. When the guard has marched in review, the commandant of the picket marches it to the left of the police guard, where it stacks its arms, and is dismissed; the arms are under charge of the sentinel of the police guard.

600. The picket does not assemble at night except in cases of alarm, or when the whole or a part is to march; then the officer of the day calls the officers, the latter the non-commissioned officers, and these the men, for which purpose each ascertains the tents of those he is to call; they are assembled without beat of drum or other noise. At night, cavalry pickets assemble mounted.

601. Pickets rejoin their companies whenever the regiment is under arms for review, drill, march, or battle.

GRAND GUARDS AND OTHER OUTPOSTS.

602. Grand guards are the advanced posts of a camp or cantonment, and should cover the approaches to it. Their number, strength, and position are regulated by the commanders of brigades; in detached corps, by the commanding officer. When it can be, the grand guards of cavalry and infantry are combined, the cavalry furnishing the advanced sentinels. When the cavalry is weak, the grand guards are infantry, but furnished with a few cavalry soldiers, to get and carry intelligence of the enemy.

603. The strength of the grand guard of a brigade will depend on its object and the strength of the regiments, the nature of the country, the position of the enemy, and the disposition of the inhabitants. It is usually commanded by a Captain.

604. Under the supervision of the Generals of Division and Brigade, the grand guards are specially under the direction of a field officer of the day in each brigade. In case of necessity, Captains may be added to the roster of Lieutenant-Colonels and Majors for this detail.

613. After a grand guard is posted, the first care of the commander and of the field officer of the day is to get news of the enemy; then to reconnoitre his position, and the roads, bridges, fords, and defiles. This reconnoissance determines the force and position of the small posts and their sentinels day and night. These posts, according to their importance, are commanded by officers or non-commissioned officers; the cavalry posts may be relieved every four or eight hours.

614. The commander of a grand guard receives detailed instructions from the General and field officer of the day of the brigade, and instructs the commanders of the small posts as to their duties and the arrangements for defense or retreat. The commanders of grand guards may, in urgent cases, change the positions of the small posts. If the small posts are to change their positions at night, they wait until the grand guard have got into position and darkness hides their movements from the enemy; then march silently and rapidly under the charge of an officer.

619. Grand guards are often charged with the care and working of telegraphic signals.

620. The sentinels and vedettes are placed on points from which they can see farthest, taking care not to break their connection with each other or with their posts. They are concealed from the enemy as much as possible by walls, or trees, or elevated ground. It is generally even of more advantage not to be seen than to see far. They should not be placed near covers, where the enemy may capture them.

621. A sentinel should always be ready to fire; vedettes carry their pistols or carbines in their hands. A sentinel must be sure of the presence of an enemy before he fires; once satisfied of that, he must fire, though all defense on his part be useless, as the safety

of the post may depend on it. Sentinels fire on all persons deserting to the enemy.

625. With raw troops, or when the light troops of the enemy are numerous or active, and when the country is broken or wooded, the night stormy or dark, sentinels should be doubled. In this case, while one watches, the other, called a flying sentinel, moves about, examining the paths and hollows.

639. Bearers of flags are not permitted to pass the outer chain of sentinels; their faces are turned from the post or army; if necessary, their eyes are bandaged; a non-commissioned officer stays with them to prevent indiscretion of the sentinels.

641. Deserters are disarmed at the advanced posts, and sent to the commander of the grand guard, who gets from them all the information he can concerning his post. If many come at night, they are received *cautiously, a few at a time.* They are sent in the morning to the field officer of the day, or to the nearest post or camp, to be conducted to the General of the brigade. All suspected persons are searched by the commanders of the posts.

642. When an enemy advances to attack, unless he is in too great force, or the grand guard is to defend an intrenched post or a defile, it will take the positions and execute the movements to check the enemy, acting as skirmishers, or fighting in close or open order, as may be best. The guard joins its corps when in line, or when a sufficient number of troops have reached the ground it defends.

RECONNOISSANCES.

656. Near an enemy, daily reconnoissances are made to observe the ground in front, and to discover whether the advanced guards of the enemy have been increased or put in motion, or any other sign of his preparation for march or action.

657. They are made by small parties of cavalry and infantry, from the brigade, under direction of the General of Division or the General of a separate brigade, and to less distance by the

patrols of the grand guard, and are not repeated at the same hour or by the same route. On the plain, reconnoissances are made by cavalry; among mountains, by infantry, with a few horsemen to carry intelligence.

658. Reconnoitring parties observe the following precautions: to leave small posts, or sentinels at intervals, to transmit intelligence to the advanced posts of the army, unless the return is to be by a different route; to march with caution, to avoid fighting; and see, if possible, without being seen; to keep an advanced guard; to send well-mounted men ahead of the advanced guard, and on the flank of the party; to instruct the scouts that no two should enter a defile or mount a hill together, but to go one at a time, while one watches to carry the news if the other is taken.

659. Before daybreak the advanced guard and scouts are drawn closer; the party then march slowly and silently, stop frequently to listen, and keep the horses that neigh in the rear. The party should enter no wood, defile, village, or inclosure, until it has been fully examined by the scouts.

660. Special reconnoissances are made under the instruction of the General in command, by such officers and with such force as he may direct.

661. Offensive or forced reconnoissances are to ascertain with certainty points in the enemy's position, or his strength. They are sometimes preludes to real actions, and sometimes only demonstrations. They drive in his outposts, and sometimes engage special corps of his line. They are only made by the order of the General commanding-in-chief, or the commander of an isolated corps.

662. In all reports of reconnoissances, the officer making them shall distinguish expressly what he has seen from the accounts he has not been able to verify personally.

663. In special and offensive reconnoissances, the report must be accompanied by a field-sketch of the localities, the dispositions and defenses of the enemy.

PARTISANS AND FLANKERS.

664. The operations of partisan corps depend on the nature and theatre of the war; they enter into the general plan of operations, and are conducted under the orders of the General commanding-in-chief.

665. The composition and strength of partisan corps and detachments of flankers depend on the object, the difficulties, the distance, and the probable time of the expedition.

666. The purpose of these isolated corps is to reconnoitre at a distance on the flanks of the army, to protect its operations, to deceive the enemy, to interrupt his communications, to intercept his couriers and his correspondence, to threaten or destroy his magazines, to carry off his posts and his convoys, or, at all events, to retard his march by making him detach largely for their protection.

667. While these corps fatigue the enemy and embarrass his operations, they endeavor to inspire confidence and secure the good will of the inhabitants in a friendly country, and to hold them in check in an enemy's country.

668. They move actively, appear unexpectedly on different points in such a manner as to make it impossible to estimate their force, or to tell whether they are irregular forces or an advanced guard.

669. These operations require vigilance, secrecy, energy, and promptness. The partisan commander must frequently supply by stratagem and audacity what he wants in numbers.

670. These detachments are sometimes composed of different arms, but the service belongs more particularly to the light cavalry, which can move to a distance by rapid marches, surprise the enemy, attack unexpectedly, and retire as promptly.

671. Stormy weather, fogs, extreme heat, and the night above all, are favorable to the success of ambuscades; when the enemy are careless, the break of day is the best time. A partisan commander should communicate to his second in command his secret orders, the direction and object of the expedition, and the different points of junction with the army.

672. Guides of the country and spies are often necessary to the partisan. They are examined separately, and confronted if their accounts differ. When there is but one guide, he marches with the advanced guard, guarded by two men, and bound if necessary. Peddlers and smugglers are specially suitable for spies.

673. A fit time to attack a convoy is at a halt, or when they begin to park, or when they are watering, or passing a wood or a defile; at a bend of the road, a bridge, or steep ascent.

674. The attacking party may be principally cavalry, with some infantry. The first object is to disperse the escort. A part of the detachment attacks the main body of the escort, another the wagons, and a third is in reserve; skirmishers line the road, and try to cut the traces, and to seize the front and rear wagons, and turn them across the road, to prevent the train from advancing or retreating.

675. If the convoy is parked, the cavalry surrounds it, assails the escort, and tries to draw it away from the train. The infantry then engage the troops remaining at the park, slip under the wagons, and get into the park. When the cavalry is alone and the enemy are shaken, they dismount a portion of the men to supply the want of infantry.

676. If it is a large convoy, the principal attack is made on the centre; the most valuable wagons are also selected, and additional horses are put to them if the attack is successful. Those that cannot be carried off are burned.

MARCHES.

677. The object of the movement and the nature of the ground determine the order of march, the kind of troops in each column, and the number of columns.

678. The force is divided into as many columns as circumstances permit, without weakening any one too much. They ought to preserve their communications, and be within supporting distance of each other. The commander of each column ought to know the strength and direction of the others.

685. Cavalry and infantry do not march together, unless the proximity of the enemy makes it necessary.

691. If possible, each column is preceded by a detachment of sappers, to remove obstacles to the march, aided, when necessary, by infantry, or the people of the country. The detachment is divided into two sections: one stops to remove the first obstacle, the other moves on to the next.

693. On the march no one shall fire a gun, or cry *"halt"* or *"march"* without orders.

694. Soldiers are not to stop for water; the canteens should be filled before starting.

697. In night marches, the Sergeant-Major of each regiment remains at the rear with a drummer, to give notice when darkness or difficulty stops the march. In cavalry, a trumpet is placed in rear of each squadron, and the signal repeated to the head of the regiment.

702. No honors are paid by troops on the march or at halts.

703. The sick march with the wagons.

705. If two corps meet on the same road, they pass to the right, and both continue their march, if the road is wide enough; if it is not, the first in the order of battle takes the road, the other halts.

706. A corps in march must not be cut by another. If two corps meet at cross-roads, that which arrives last halts if the other is in motion. A corps in march passes a corps at a halt, if it has precedence in the order of battle, or if the halted corps is not ready to move at once.

JOURNAL.

708. Commanding officers of troops marching through a country little known, will keep journals of their marches according to the form and directions hereto annexed. At the end of the march a copy of the journal will be retained at the station where the troops arrive, and the original will be forwarded to the head-

quarters of the Department, or *corps d'armée*. Thence, after a copy has been taken, it will be transmitted, through the head-quarters of the army, to the Adjutant-General, for the information of the War Department.

POSTS.

716. Whenever a new post is established, or a camp, meant to be occupied for some time, the commanding officer will forward to the Adjutant-General's office, as well as to the head-quarters of the Department, or *corps d'armée* if in the field, an accurate description of its locality, of its distance and bearings from the nearest known point, and the manner of reaching it by mail, together with a sketch of the country in its immediate vicinity.

717. Military posts will be named by the Secretary of War.

BATTLES.

718. Dispositions for battle depend on the number, kind, and quality of the troops opposed, on the ground, and on the objects of the war; but the following rules are to be observed generally:

719. In attacking, the advanced guard endeavors to capture the enemy's outposts, or cut them off from the main body. Having done so, or driven them in, it occupies, in advancing, all the points that can cover or facilitate the march of the army, or secure its retreat, such as bridges, defiles, woods, and heights; it then makes attacks, to occupy the enemy, without risking too much, and to deceive them as to the march and projects of the army.

722. At proper distance from the enemy, the troops are formed for the attack in several lines; if only two can be formed, some battalions in column are placed behind the wings of the second line. The lines may be formed of troops in column or in order of battle, according to the ground and plan of attack.

724. The reserve is formed of the best troops of foot and horse, to complete a victory or make good a retreat. It is placed in the rear of the centre, or chief point of attack or defense.

725. The cavalry should be distributed in echelon on the wings and at the centre, on favorable ground.

727. In the attack, the artillery is employed to silence the batteries that protect the position. In the defense, it is better to direct its fire on the advancing troops. In either case, as many pieces are united as possible, the fire of artillery being formidable in proportion to its concentration.

732. When a success is gained, the light troops should pursue the enemy promptly and rapidly. The other troops will restore order in their columns, then advance from position to position, always prepared for an attack or to support the troops engaged.

733. Before the action, the Generals indicate the places where they will be; if they change position, they give notice of it, or leave a staff officer to show where they have gone.

734. During the fight the officers and non-commissioned officers keep the men in the ranks, and enforce obedience if necessary. Soldiers must not be permitted to leave the ranks to strip or rob the dead,—nor even to assist the wounded unless by express permission, which is only to be given after the action is decided. The highest interest and most pressing duty is to win the victory, by winning which only can a proper care of the wounded be ensured.

735. Before the action, the Quartermaster of the division makes all the necessary arrangements for the transportation of the wounded. He establishes the ambulance depôts in the rear, and gives his assistants the necessary instructions for the service of the ambulance wagons and other means of removing the wounded.

736. The ambulance depôt, to which the wounded are carried or directed for immediate treatment, is generally established at the most convenient building nearest the field of battle. A *red flag* marks its place, or the way to it, to the conductors of the ambulances and to the wounded who can walk.

737. The active ambulances follow the troops engaged to succor the wounded and remove them to the depôts; for this

purpose the conductors should always have the necessary assistants, that the soldiers may have no excuse to leave the ranks for that object.

740. The wounded in the depôts and the sick are removed, as soon as possible, to the hospitals that have been established by the Quartermaster-General of the army on the flanks or rear of the army.

741. After an action, the officers of ordnance collect the munitions of war left on the field, and make a return of them to the General. The Quartermaster's Department collects the rest of the public property captured, and makes the returns to head-quarters.

742. Written reports for the General commanding-in-chief are made by commandants of regiments, batteries, and separate squadrons, and by all commanders of a higher grade, each in what concerns his own command, and to his immediate commander.

743. When an officer or soldier deserves mention for conduct in action, a special report shall be made in his case, and the General commanding-in-chief decides whether to mention him in his report to the government and in his orders. But he shall not be mentioned in the report until he has been mentioned in the orders to the army. These special reports are examined with care by the intermediate commanders, to verify the facts, and secure commendation and rewards to the meritorious only.

744. The report of battles, which must frequently be made before these special reports of persons are scrutinized, is confined to general praise or blame, and an account of the operations.

PRISONERS OF WAR.

745. Prisoners of war will be disarmed and sent to the rear, and reported as soon as practicable to the head-quarters. The return of prisoners from the Head-Quarters of the Army to the War Department will specify the number, rank, and corps.

746. The private property of prisoners will be duly respected, and each shall be treated with the regard due to his rank. They

are to obey the necessary orders given them. They receive for subsistence one ration each, without regard to rank; and the wounded are to be treated with the same care as the wounded of the army. Other allowances to them will depend on conventions with the enemy. Prisoners' horses will be taken for the army.

747. Exchanges of prisoners and release of officers on parole depend on the orders of the General commanding-in-chief, under the instructions of government.

CONVOYS AND THEIR ESCORTS.

748. The strength and composition of the escort of a convoy depend on the country, the nature and value of the convoy, and the dangers it may incur. A larger escort is required for a convoy of powder, that the defense may not be near the train.

749. Cavalry is employed in escorts chiefly to reconnoitre; the proportion is larger as the country is more open.

750. Pioneers or working-parties are attached to convoys to mend roads, remove obstacles, and erect defenses. The convoys should always be provided with spare wheels, poles, axles, &c.

751. The commandant of the escort should receive detailed instructions in writing.

753. Officers who accompany the convoy, but do not belong to the escort, shall exercise no authority in it except by consent of the commander. If these officers are junior to the commander, he may assign them to duty if the defense requires it.

755. Generally, munitions of war are at the head of the convoy, subsistence next, and then other military stores; the sutler last. But always that part of the convoy which is most important to the army shall be where it is most secure from danger.

756. The commandant should send out reconnoitering parties, and never put the convoy in motion until their reports have been received. He always forms an advance and rear guard, and keeps the main body under his immediate order at the most important point, with small guards or posts at other points.

757. In an open country the main body marches by the side of the road, opposite the centre of the convoy; in other cases at the head or rear of the column, as the one or the other is most exposed.

758. The advance guard precedes the convoy far enough to remove all obstacles to its advance. It examines the woods, defiles, and villages, and by mounted men gives information to the commander, and receives his orders. It reconnoitres places for halts and parks.

762. If the convoy is large, and has to pass places that the force and position of the enemy make dangerous, the loss of the whole convoy must not be risked; it must pass by divisions, which reunite after the passage. In this case, the greater part of the troops guard the first division; they seize the important points, and cover them until all the divisions have passed.

763. If there is artillery in the convoy, the commander of the escort uses it for the defense.

764. To move faster and make the defense easier, the wagons move in double file whenever the road allows it. If a wagon breaks, it is at once removed from the road; when repaired, it takes the rear; when it cannot be repaired, its load and horses are distributed so some of the other wagons kept in the rear for that purpose.

766. Convoys halt every hour to let the horses take breath and the wagons close up. Long halts are made but seldom, and only in places that have been reconnoitred and found favorable for defense. At night the park is arranged for defense, and in preference at a distance from inhabited places, if in an enemy's country.

767. The wagons are usually parked in ranks, axle against axle, the poles in the same direction, and with sufficient space between the ranks for the horses. If an attack is feared, they are parked in square, the hind-wheels outside, and the horses inside.

768. On the appearance of the enemy during the march, the commander closes up the wagons and continues his march in order; he avoids fighting; but if the enemy seizes a position that

commands his road, he attacks vigorously with the mass of his force, but is not to continue the pursuit far from the convoy. The convoy halts, and resumes the march when the position is carried.

769. When the enemy is too strong to be attacked, the convoy is parked in square if there is room; if not, closed up in double file; at the front and rear the road is blocked by wagons across it. The drivers are dismounted at the heads of the horses. They are not permitted to make their escape. The light troops keep the enemy at a distance as long as possible, and are supported when necessary, but prudently, as the troops must be kept in hand to resist the main attack.

770. If a wagon takes fire in the park, remove it if possible; if not, remove first the ammunition wagons, then those leeward of the fire.

771. When a whole convoy cannot be saved, the most valuable part may sometimes be by abandoning the rest. If all efforts fail, and there is no hope of succor, the convoy must be set on fire and the horses killed that cannot be saved; the escort may then cut its way through.

772. If the convoy is of prisoners of war, every effort should be made to reach a village or strong building where they may be confined; if forced to fight in the field, the prisoners must be secured and made to lie down until the action is over.

BAGGAGE TRAINS.

773. The baggage train of general head-quarters and the trains of the several divisions are each under the charge of an officer of the Quartermaster's Department. These officers command and conduct the trains under the orders they receive from their respective head-quarters. When the trains of different divisions march together, or the train of a division marches with the train of general head-quarters, the senior Quartermaster directs the whole.

774. The Regimental Quartermaster has charge of the wagons, horses, equipments, and all means of transport employed in

the service of the regiment. Under the orders of the Colonel, he assembles them for the march and maintains the order and police of the train in park and on the march. On marches, the regimental trains are under the orders of the Quartermaster of the division. When the march is by brigade, the senior Regimental Quartermaster in the brigade, or the Quartermaster of the brigade, has the direction of the whole. The necessary wagon-masters, or non-commissioned officers to act as such, are employed with the several trains.

776. When the train of head-quarters is to have a guard, the strength of the guard is regulated by the General. When the guard of a train is the escort for its defense, the regulations in regard to convoys and escorts take effect.

778. The wagon-masters, under the orders of the officers of the Quartermaster's Department, exercise the necessary restraints over the teamsters and servants who leave their teams, or do not properly conduct them; or who ill treat their horses, or who attempt to pillage, or run away in case of attack.

779. The General commanding the army and the Generals of Division will not permit any general or staff officer, or regiment under their orders, or any person whatsoever, attached to their command, to have more than the authorized amount or means of transportation. For this purpose they will themselves make, and cause to be made, frequent reviews and inspections of the trains. They will see that no trooper is employed to lead [a] private horse, no soldier to drive a private vehicle, and that no trooper [is] put on foot to lead his horse to an officer. They will not permit the wagons of the artillery or of the train to be loaded with any thing foreign to their proper service, nor any public horse, for any occasion, to be harnessed to a private carriage.

GENERAL POLICE.

781. When necessary, the General-in-chief or General of Division may appoint a provost marshal to take charge of prisoners, with a suitable guard, or other police force.

782. Private servants, not soldiers, will not be allowed to wear the uniform of any corps of the army, but each will be required to carry with him a certificate from the officer who employs him, verified, for regimental officers, by the signature of the Colonel; for other officers under the rank of Colonel, by the chief of their corps or department.

783. Laundresses permitted to follow the army will be furnished with certificates, signed as in the preceding paragraph, and no woman of bad character will be allowed to follow the army. Other persons with the army, not officers or soldiers, such as guides of the country, interpreters, &c., will carry about them similar certificates from the head-quarters that employs them.

784. Deserters from the enemy, after being examined, will be secured for some days, as they may be spies in disguise; as opportunities offer, they will be sent to the rear; after which, if they are found lurking about the army, or attempting to return to the enemy, they will be treated with severity.

785. The arms and accoutrements of deserters will be turned over to the Ordnance Department, and their horses to the corps in want of them, after being branded with the letters "U.S." The compensation to be accorded to deserters, for such objects, will be according to appraisement, made under the directive of the Quartermaster's Department. The enlistment of deserters, without express permission from general head-quarters, is prohibited.

786. It is forbidden to purchase horses without ascertaining the right of the party to sell. Stolen horses shall be restored. Estrays, in the enemy's country, when the owner is not discovered, are taken for the army.

787. Plundering and marauding, at all times disgraceful to soldiers, when committed on the persons or property of those whom it is the duty of the army to protect, become crimes of such enormity as to admit of no remission of the lawful punishment which the military law awards against offenses of this nature.

SAFEGUARDS.

788. Safeguards are protections granted to persons or property in foreign parts by the commanding general, or by other commanders within the limits of their command.

789. Safeguards are usually given to protect hospitals, public establishments, establishments of religion, charity, or instruction, museums, depositories of the arts, mills, post-offices, and other institutions of public benefit; also to individuals whom it may be the interest of the army to respect.

790. A safeguard may consist of one or more men of fidelity and firmness, generally non-effective non-commissioned officers, furnished with a paper setting out clearly the protection and exemptions it is intended to secure, signed by the commander giving it, and his staff officer; or it may consist of such paper, delivered to the part whose person, family, house, and property it is designed to protect. These safeguards must be numbered and registered.

791. The men left as safeguards by one corps may be replaced by another. They are withdrawn when the country is evacuated; but if not, they have orders to await the arrival of the enemy's troops, and apply to the commander for a safe-conduct to the outposts.

55th Article of the Rules and Articles of War

"Whosoever belonging to the armies of the United States, employed in foreign parts, shall force a safeguard, shall suffer death."

SIEGES.

793. In the following regulations the besieging force is supposed to be two divisions of infantry and a brigade of cavalry. The same principles govern in other cases.

802. The divisions, brigades, regiments, and battalions are encamped during the siege in the order of battle. The service of camp is conducted as heretofore prescribed.

803. The infantry has two kinds of siege service,—the guard of the trenches and the work of the trenches.

809. The battalions first for detail for guard of the trenches, and the companies first for detail for work in the trenches, furnish no other details, and are held on picket, ready to march at the call of the field officer of the trenches.

810. Materials for the siege, such as fascines, gabions, hurdles, pickets, &c., are furnished by the different corps, in the proportion ordered by the General.

811. Guards and workmen going to the trenches march without beat of drum or music.

812. At all times, and especially on the day the trenches are opened, everything is avoided likely to attract the attention of the enemy. With this view, the General may vary the hour of relieving guards.

820. No honors are paid in the trenches. When the General commanding the siege visits them, the guards place themselves in rear of the banquette, and rest on their arms. The colors are never carried to the trenches unless the whole regiment marches to repulse a sortie or make an assault. Even in this case they are not displayed until the General commanding the siege gives the order.

826. When it is necessary to dismount cavalry and send them to the trenches, they should be employed as near their camp as possible, and posted between detachments of infantry.

827. Men belonging to the cavalry may, in assaults, be employed in carrying fascines and other materials to fill ditches and make passages.

828. The general officers of cavalry are more particularly employed in the service of posts and detachments placed in observation to protect the siege. They and the field officers of this arm are employed in the command of escorts to convoys, or whatever arms the escorts may be composed. When these duties are not sufficient to employ them, they take their share of the duty in the trenches.

832. However practicable the breach may appear, or however, ruined the works in rear of it, the heads of columns must always be supplied with ladders to get over unexpected obstacles.

833. The General commanding the siege designates picked companies to protect property and persons, and prevent pillage and violence, from the moment the place is carried. The officers exert themselves to restrain the men.

835. Whether the place is taken by assault or by capitulation, the provisions and military stores, and the public funds, are reserved for the use of the army.

DEFENSE OF FORTIFIED PLACES.

839. In war, every commander of a fortified place shall always hold himself prepared with his plan of defense, as if at any time liable to attack. He arranges this plan according to the probable mode of attack; determines the posts of the troops in the several parts of the works, the reliefs, the reserves, and the details of service in all the corps. He draws up instructions for a case of attack, and exercises the garrison according to his plan of defense. In sea-coast works, he provides the instructions for the different batteries on the approach of ships.

841. On the approach of an enemy, he removes all houses and other objects, within or without the place, that cover the approaches, or interrupt the fire of the guns or the movements of the troops. He assures himself personally that all posterns, outlets, embrasures, &c., are in proper state of security.

846. The commander shall defend in succession the advanced works, the covered way and outworks, the body of the work, and the interior intrenchments. He will not be content with clearing away the foot of the breaches, and defending them by abattis, mines, and all other means used in sieges; but he shall begin in good time, behind the bastions or front of attack, the necessary intrenchments to resist assaults on the main work.

849. When the commander thinks that the end of the defense has come, he shall still consult the council of defense on the means that may remain to prolong the siege. But in all cases he alone will decide on the time, manner, and terms of surrender. In the capitulation, he shall not seek or accept better terms for himself than for the garrison, but shall share their fate, and exert his best endeavors for the care of the troops, and especially of the sick and wounded.

850. No commander in the field shall withdraw troops or supplies from any fortified place, or exercise any authority over its commandant, unless it has been put subject to his orders by competent authority.

ARTICLE XXXVII.

TROOPS ON BOARD OF TRANSPORTS.

851. Military commanders charged with the embarkation of troops, and officers of the Quartermaster's Department intrusted with the selection of the transports, will take care that the vessels are entirely seaworthy and proper for such service, and that suitable arrangements are made in them for the health and comfort of the troops.

852. If, in the opinion of the officer commanding the troops to be embarked, the vessel is not proper or suitably arranged, the officer charged with the embarkation shall cause her to be inspected by competent and experienced persons.

854. Arms will be so placed, if there be no racks, as to be secure from injury, and enable the men to handle them promptly—bayonets unfixed and in scabbard.

855. Ammunition in cartridge-boxes to be so placed as to be entirely secure from fire; reserve ammunition to be reported to the master of the transport, with request that he designate a safe place of deposit. Frequent inspections will be made of the service ammunition, to insure its safety and good condition.

856. No officer is to sleep out of his ship, or to quit his ship, without the sanction of the officer commanding on board.

857. The guard will be proportioned to the number of sentinels required. At sea the guard will mount with side-arms only. The officer of the guard will be officer of the day.

858. Sentinels will be kept over the fires, with buckets of water at hand, promptly to extinguish fires. Smoking is prohibited *between decks or in the cabins*, at all times; nor shall any lights be allowed between decks, except such ship lanterns as the master of the transport may direct, or those carried by the officer of the day in the execution of his duty.

861. All the troops will turn out at ———, A.M., without arms or uniform, and (in warm weather) without shoes or stockings; when every individual will be clean, his hands, face, and feet washed, and his hair combed. The same personal inspection will be repeated thirty minutes before sunset. The cooks alone may be exempted from *one* of these inspections per day, if necessary.

862. Recruits or awkward men will be exercised in the morning and evening in the use of arms, an hour each time, when the weather will permit.

863. Officers will enforce cleanliness as indispensable to health. When the weather will permit, bedding will be brought on deck every morning for airing. Tubs may be fixed on the forecastle for bathing, or the men may be placed in the *chains* and have buckets of water thrown over them.

871. At morning and evening parades, the Surgeon will examine the men, to observe whether there be any appearance of disease.

875. In harbor, where there is no danger from sharks, the men may bathe; but not more than ten at a time, and attended by a boat.

876. In fitting up a vessel for the transportation of horses, care is to be taken that the requisite arrangements are made for conveniently feeding and cleaning them, and to secure them from injury in rough weather by ropes attached to breast-straps and

breeching, or by other suitable means; and especially that proper ventilation is provided by openings in the upper deck, wind-sails, &c. The ventilation of steamers may be assisted by using the engine for that purpose.

877. Horses should not be put on board after severe exercise or when heated. In hoisting them on board, the slings should be made fast to a hook at the end of the fall, or the knot tied by an expert seaman, so that it may be well secured yet easily loosened. The horse should be run up quickly, to prevent him from plunging, and should be steadied by guide ropes. A halter is placed on him before he is lifted from the ground.

878. On board, care is to be taken that the horses are not over-fed; bran should form part of their ration. The face, eyes, and nostrils of each horse are to be washed at the usual stable hours, and, occasionally, the mangers should be washed and the nostrils of the horses sponged with vinegar and water.

ARTICLE XXXVIII.

COURTS-MARTIAL.

880. In appointing a general court-martial, as many members will be detailed, from five to thirteen inclusively, as can be assembled without manifest injury to the service.

881. The decision of the officer appointing the court, as to the number that can be assembled without manifest injury to the service, is conclusive.

882. A President of the court will not be appointed. The officer highest in rank present will be President.

883. Form of Order appointing a general court-martial; the last paragraph omitted when the court can be kept up with thirteen members.

Head-Quarters, ———, &c.

A General Court-martial is hereby appointed to meet at ———, on the — day of ———, or as soon thereafter as practicable, for the trial of ——— and such other prisoners as may be brought before it.

Detail for the Court:

1. ———	8. ———
2. ———	9. ———
3. ———	10. ———
4. ———	11. ———
5. ———	12. ———
6. ———	13. ———
7. ———	—— ——, Judge Advocate.

No other officers than those named can be assembled without manifest injury to the service.

By order of —— ——, commanding ——.

—— ——, Assistant Adjutant-General.

884. In the detail the members will be named, and they will take place in the court, in the order of their rank. A decision of the proper authority in regard to the rank of the members cannot be reversed by the court.

885. The place of holding a court is appointed by the authority convening it.

886. Application for delay or postponement of trial must, when practicable, be made to the authority convening the court. When made to the court, it must be before plea, and will then, if in the opinion of the court well founded, be referred to the authority convening the court, to decide whether the court should be adjourned or dissolved, and the charges reserved for another court.

887. Upon application by the accused for postponement on the ground of the absence of a witness, it ought distinctly to appear on his oath, 1st. that the witness is material, and how; 2d. that the accused has used due diligence to procure his atten-

dance; and, 3d. that he has reasonable ground to believe, and does believe, that he will be able to procure such attendance within a reasonable time stated.

888. The President of a court-martial, besides his duties and privileges as member, is the organ of the court, to keep order and conduct its business. He speaks and acts for the court in each case where the rule has been prescribed by law, regulation, or its own resolution. In all their Deliberations the law secures the equality of the members.

889. The 76th Article of War does not confer on a court-martial the power to punish its own members. For disorderly conduct, a member is liable as in other offenses against military discipline; improper words are to be taken down, and any disorderly conduct of a member reported to the authority convening the court.

890. The Judge Advocate shall summon the necessary witnesses for the trial; but he shall not summon any witness at the expense of the United States, nor any officer of the army, without the order of the court, unless satisfied that his testimony is material and necessary to the ends of justice.

891. Every court-martial shall keep a complete and accurate record of its proceedings, to be authenticated by the signatures of the President and Judge Advocate; who shall also certify, in like manner, the sentence pronounced by the court in each case. The record must show that the court was organized as the law requires; that the court and Judge Advocate were duly sworn in the presence of the prisoner; that he was previously asked whether he had any objection to any member, and his answer thereto. A copy of the order appointing the court will be entered on the record in each case.

892. Whenever the same court-martial tries more prisoners than one, and they are arraigned on separate and distinct charges, the court is to be sworn at the commencement of each trial, and the proceedings in each case will be made up separately.

894. No recommendation will be embraced in the body of the sentence. Those members only who concur in the recommendation will sign it.

895. The legal punishments for soldiers by sentence of a court-martial according to the offense, and the jurisdiction of the court, are—death; confinement; confinement on bread and water diet; solitary confinement; hard labor; ball and chain; forfeiture of pay and allowances; discharges from service; and reprimands, and, when non-commissioned officers, reduction to the ranks. Ordnance Sergeants and Hospital Stewards, however, though liable to discharge, may not be reduced. Nor are they to be tried by regimental or garrison courts-martial, unless by special permission of the department commander. Solitary confinement, or confinement on bread and water, shall not exceed fourteen days at a time, with intervals between the periods of such confinement not less than such periods; and not exceeding eighty-four days in any one year.

896. The Judge Advocate shall transmit the proceedings, without delay, to the officer having authority to confirm the sentence, who shall state, at the end of the proceedings in each case, his decision and orders thereon.

897. The original proceedings of all general courts-martial, after the decision on them of the reviewing authority, and all proceedings that require the decision of the President under the 65th and 89th Articles of War, and copies of all orders confirming or disapproving, or remitting, the sentences of courts-martial, and all official communications for the Judge Advocate of the army, will be addressed to *The Adjutant-General of the Army, War Department,* marked on the cover, *"Judge Advocate."*

898. The proceedings of garrison and regimental courts-martial will be transmitted without delay by the garrison or regimental commander to the department head-quarters for the supervision of the department commander.

899. The power to pardon or mitigate the punishment ordered by a court-martial is vested in the authority confirming the proceedings, and in the President of the United States. A superior military commander to the officer confirming the proceedings may suspend the execution of the sentence when, in his judgment, it is void upon the face of the proceedings, or when he

sees a fit case for executive clemency. In such cases, the record, with his order prohibiting the execution, shall be transmitted for the final orders of the President.

900. When a court-martial or court of inquiry adjourns without day, the members will return to their respective posts and duties unless otherwise ordered.

901. When a court adjourns for three days, the Judge Advocate shall report the fact to the commander of the post or troops, and the members belonging to the command will be liable to duty during the time.

ARTICLE XXXIX.

WORKING-PARTIES.

902. When it is necessary to employ the army at work on fortifications, in surveys, in cutting roads, and other constant labor of not less than ten days, the non-commissioned officers and soldiers so employed are enrolled as extra-duty men, and are allowed twenty-five cents a day when employed as laborers and teamsters, and forty cents a day when employed as mechanics, clerks, storekeepers, &c., at all stations east of the Rocky Mountains, and thirty-five and fifty cents per day, respectively, at all stations west of those mountains. But no man shall be rated and paid as a clerk or mechanic, who is not *skilled* in his particular employment; nor any man as a storekeeper, &c., whose trust is not of sufficient importance. Mere strikers, inferior workmen, &c. shall be rated as *laborers*. Commanding officers will particularly see to this; nor shall any soldier be rated at the higher pay, except by their order.

903. Enlisted men of the Ordnance and Engineer Departments, and artificers of artillery, are not entitled to this allowance when employed in their appropriate work.

904. Soldiers will not be employed as extra-duty men for any labor in camp or garrison which can properly be performed by fatigue parties.

908. The officer commanding a working-party will conform to the directions and plans of the engineer or other officer directing the work, without regard to rank.

909. A day's work shall not exceed ten hours in summer, nor eight in winter. Soldiers are paid in proportion for any greater number of hours they are employed each day. Summer is considered to commence on the 1st of April, and winter on the 1st of October.

910. Although the necessities of the service may require soldiers to be ordered on working-parties as a duty, commanding officers are to bear in mind that fitness for military service by instruction and discipline is the object for which the army is kept on foot, and that they are not to employ the troops when not in the field, and especially the mounted troops, in labors that interfere with their military duties and exercises, except in case of immediate necessity, which shall be forthwith reported for the orders of the War Department.

ARTICLE XL.

RECRUITING SERVICE.

911. The recruiting service will be conducted by the Adjutant-General, under the direction of the Secretary of War.

912. Field officers will be detailed to superintend the recruiting districts, and lieutenants to take charge of the recruiting parties. The Adjutant-General will select the field officers, and announce in orders the number of Captains and Lieutenants to be selected for this duty from each regiment by the Colonel.

913. A recruiting party will consist generally of one lieutenant, one non-commissioned officer, two privates, and a drummer and fifer. The parties will be sent from the principal depôts, and none but suitable men selected.

914. Officers on the general recruiting service are not to be ordered on any other duty, except from the Adjutant-General's office.

DUTIES OF RECRUITING OFFICERS.

925. Success in obtaining recruits depends much on the activity and *personal attention* of recruiting officers, and they will not entrust to enlisted men the duties for which themselves only are responsible. They will in no case absent themselves from their stations without authority from the superintendent.

926. They will not allow any man to be deceived or inveigled into the service by false representations, but will in person explain the nature of the service, the length of the term, the pay, clothing, rations, and other allowances to which a soldier is entitled by law, to every man before he signs the enlistment.

927. If minors present themselves, they are to be treated with great candor; the names and residences of their parents or guardians, if they have any, must be ascertained, and these will be informed of the minor's wish to enlist, that they may make their objections or give their consent.

928. With the sanction of superintendents, recruiting officers may insert, in not exceeding two newspapers, brief notices directing attention to the rendezvous for further information.

929. Any free white male person above the age of eighteen and under thirty-five years, being at least five feet three inches high, effective, able-bodied, sober, free from disease, of good character and habits, and with a competent knowledge of the English language, may be enlisted. This regulation, so far as respects the *height* and *age* of the recruit, shall not extend to musicians or to soldiers who may *"re-enlist,"* or have served honestly and faithfully a previous enlistment in the army.

930. No man having a wife or child shall be enlisted *in time of peace* without special authority obtained from the Adjutant-General's Office, through the superintendent. This rule is not to apply to soldiers who *"re-enlist."*

931. No person under the age of twenty-one years is to be enlisted or re-enlisted without the written consent of his parent, guardian, or master. The recruiting officers must be very particular in ascertaining the true age of the recruit.

932. After the nature of the service and terms of enlistment have been fairly explained to the recruit, the officer, before the enlistments are filled up, will read to him, and offer for his signature, the annexed declaration, to be appended to each copy of his enlistment:

I, ———, desiring to enlist in the Army of the United States for the period of five years, do declare that I am ——— years and ——— months of age; that I have neither wife nor child; that I have never been discharged from the United States service on account of disability, or by sentence of a court-martial, or by order before the expiration of a term of enlistment; and I know of no impediment to my serving honestly and faithfully as a soldier for five years.

Witness: ——————————

—————————

933. If the recruit be a minor, his parent, guardian, or master must sign a consent to his enlisting, which will be added to the preceding declaration, in the following form:

I, ———, do certify that I am the (*father, only surviving parent, legal master, or guardian, as the case may be*) of ——; that the said —— is —— years of age; and I do hereby freely give my consent to his enlisting as a soldier in the Army of the United States for the period of five years.

Witness: ——————————

—————————

934. The forms of declaration, and of consent in case of a minor, having been signed and witnessed, the recruit will then be duly examined by the recruiting officer, and surgeon if one be present, and, if accepted, the 20th and 87th Articles of War will be read to him; after which he will be allowed time to consider the subject until his mind appears to be fully made up before the oath is administered to him.

935. As soon as practicable, and at least within six days after his enlistment, the following oath will be administered to the recruit:

"I, A— B—, do solemnly swear or affirm (as the case may be) that I will bear true allegiance to the United States of America, and that I will serve them honestly and faithfully against all their enemies or opposers whatsoever, and observe and obey the orders of the President of the United States, and the orders of the officers appointed over me, according to the rules and articles for the government of the armies of the United States." (See 10th Art. of War.)

936. Under the 11th section of the act of 3d August, 1861, chap. 42, the oath of enlistment and re-enlistment may be administered by any commissioned officer of the army.

937. It is the duty of the recruiting officer to be present at the examination of the recruit by the medical officer. (See par. 1261.)

938. Recruiting officers will not employ private physicians without authority from the Adjutant-General's Office, for the special purpose of examining the recruits prior to their enlisting.

946. Recruits will be sent from rendezvous to depôts every ten days, or oftener if practicable, provided the number disposable exceeds three. The detachments of recruits will be sent from rendezvous to depôts under charge of a non-commissioned officer.

DEPÔTS FOR COLLECTING AND INSTRUCTING RECRUITS.

964. The depôts for recruits are established by orders from the Adjutant-General's Office.

965. To each *depôt* there will be assigned a suitable number of officers to command and instruct the recruits; and, when necessary, such number of enlisted men as may be designated at the Adjutant-General's Office, will be selected for the permanent party, to do garrison duty and for drill-masters.

966. The number of recruits at depôts to be assigned to each arm and regiment is directed from the Adjutant-General's Office.

967. The recruits are to be *dressed in uniform* according to their respective arms, and will be regularly mustered and inspected. They are to be well drilled in the Infantry Tactics, through the school of the soldier to that of the battalion, and in

the exercise of field and garrison pieces. Duty is to be done according to the strict rules of service.

968. The general superintendent will cause such of the recruits as are found to possess a natural talent for music, to be instructed (besides the drill of the soldier) on the fife, bugle, and drum, and other military instruments; and boys of twelve years of age, and upward, may, under his direction, be enlisted for this purpose. But as recruits under eighteen years of age and under size must be discharged, if they are not capable of learning music, care should be taken to enlist those only who have a natural talent for music, and, if practicable, they should be taken on trial for some time before being enlisted.

969. Regiments will be furnished with field music on the requisitions of their commanders, made, from time to time, direct on the general superintendent; and, when requested by regimental commanders, the superintendents will endeavor to have suitable men selected from the recruits, or enlisted, for the regimental bands.

970. At every depôt pains will be taken to form from the permanent party a body of competent cooks, some of whom will be sent with every large draft of recruits ordered to regiments.

971. To give encouragement to the recruits, and hold out inducements to good conduct, the commanding officer of the depôt may promote such of them as exhibit the requisite qualifications to be *lance corporals* and *lance sergeants*, not exceeding the proper proportion to the number of recruits at the depôt. These appointments will be announced in orders in the usual way, and will be continued in force until they join their regiments, unless sooner revoked. No allowance of pay or emoluments is to be assigned to these appointments: they are only to be considered as recommendations to the captains of companies and colonels of regiments for the places in which the recruits may have acted; but such non-commissioned officers are to be treated with all the respect and to have all the authority which may belong to the stations of sergeant and corporal.

972. *Permanent* parties at depôts, and *recruiting parties* and recruits, will be mustered, inspected, and paid in the same manner as other soldiers. Recruits will be mustered for pay only at depôts, and, when paid there, one-half of their monthly pay will be retained until they join their regiments.

973. When recruits are received at a garrisoned post, the commanding officer will place them under the charge of a commissioned officer.

974. Recruits are not to be put to any labor or work which would interfere with their instruction, nor are they to be employed otherwise than as soldiers, in the regular duties of garrison and camp.

975. The Rules and Articles of War are to be read to the recruits every month, after the inspection; and so much thereof as relates to the duties of non-commissioned officers and soldiers will be read to them every week.

REGIMENTAL RECRUITING SERVICE.

985. The regimental recruiting will be conducted in the manner prescribed for the general service.

986. Every commander of a regiment is the superintendent of the recruiting service for his regiment, and will endeavor to keep it up to its establishment; for which purpose he will obtain the necessary funds, clothing, &c., by requisition on the Adjutant-General.

987. At every station occupied by his regiment, or any part of it, the colonel will designate a suitable officer to attend to the recruiting duties; which selection will not relieve such officer from his company or other ordinary duties. The officer thus designated will be kept constantly furnished with funds, and, when necessary, with clothing and camp equipage.

988. The regimental recruiting officer will, with the approbation of the commanding officer of the station, enlist all suitable men. He will be governed, in rendering his accounts and returns,

by the rules prescribed for the general service; and, when leaving a post, will turn over the funds in his hands to the senior company officer of his regiment present, unless some other be appointed to receive them.

ARTICLE XLI.

PUBLIC PROPERTY, MONEY, AND ACCOUNTS.

989. All officers of the Pay, Commissary, and Quartermaster's Departments, and military store-keepers, shall, previous to their entering on the duties of their respective offices, give good and sufficient bonds to the United States fully to account for all moneys and public property which they may receive, in such sums as the Secretary of War shall direct; and the officers aforesaid shall renew their bonds every four years, and oftener if the Secretary of War shall so require, and whenever they receive a new commission or appointment.

994. No disbursing officer shall accept, or receive, or transmit to the Treasury to be allowed in his favor, any receipt or voucher from a creditor of the United States without having paid to such creditor, in such funds as he received for disbursement, or such other funds as he is authorized by the preceding article to take in exchange, the full amount specified in such receipt or voucher; and every such act shall be deemed to be a conversion to his own use of the amount specified in such receipt or voucher. And no officer in the military service charged with the safe-keeping, transfer, or disbursement of public money, shall convert to his own use, or invest in any kind of merchandise or property, or loan with or without interest, or deposit in any bank, or exchange for other funds, except as allowed in the preceding article, any public money intrusted to him; and every such act shall be deemed to be a felony and an embezzlement of so much money as may be so taken, converted, invested, used, loaned, deposited, or exchanged. (Act August 6, 1846.)

1000. No officer disbursing or directing the disbursement of money for the military service shall be concerned, directly or indirectly, in the purchase or sale, for commercial purposes, of any article intended for, making a part of, or appertaining to the department of the public service in which he is engaged, nor shall take, receive, or apply to his own use any gain or emolument, under the guise of presents or otherwise, for negotiating or transacting any public business, other than what is or may be allowed by law.

1001. No wagon-master or forage-master shall be interested or concerned, directly or indirectly, in any wagon or other means of transport employed by the United States, nor in the purchase or sale of any property procured for or belonging to the United States, except as the agent of the United States.

1003. No person in the military service whose salary, pay, or emoluments is or are fixed by law or regulations, shall receive any additional pay, extra allowance, or compensation in any form whatever, for the disbursement of public money, or any other service or duty whatsoever, unless the same shall be authorized by law, and explicitly set out in the appropriation.

1016. Public horses, mules, oxen, tools, and implements shall be branded conspicuously U. S. before being used in service, and all other public property that it may be useful to mark; and all public property having the brand of the U. S. when sold or condemned, shall be branded with the letter C.

1017. No public property shall be used, nor labor hired for the public be employed, for any private use whatsoever not authorized by the regulations of the service.

1040. Every officer intrusted with public money or property shall render all prescribed returns and accounts to the bureau of the department in which he is serving, where all such returns and accounts shall pass through a rigid administrative scrutiny before the money accounts are transmitted to the proper offices of the Treasury Department for settlement.

1053. It is the duty of every commanding officer to enforce a rigid economy in the public expenses.

SIGNAL OFFICER.

1063. The signal officer shall have charge, under the direction of the Secretary of War, of all signal duty, and of all books, papers, and apparatus connected therewith.

ARTICLE XLII.

QUARTERMASTER'S DEPARTMENT.

1064. This department provides the quarters and transportation of the army; storage and transportation for all army supplies; army clothing; camp and garrison equipage; cavalry and artillery horses; fuel; forage; straw; material for bedding, and stationery.

1065. The incidental expenses of the army paid through the Quartermaster's Department include per diem to extra-duty men; postage on public service; the expenses of courts-martial, of the pursuit and apprehension of deserters, of the burials of officers and soldiers, of hired escorts, of expresses, interpreters, spies, and guides, of veterinary surgeons and medicines for horses, and of supplying posts with water; and generally the proper and authorized expenses for the movements and operations of an army not expressly assigned to any other department.

BARRACKS AND QUARTERS.

1066. Under this head are included the permanent buildings for the use of the army, as barracks, quarters, hospitals, store-houses, offices, stables.

1067. When barracks and quarters are to be occupied, they will be allotted by the quartermaster at the station, under the control of the commanding officer.

1068. The number of rooms and amount of fuel for officers and men are as follows:

	Rooms.			Cords of wood per month.[*]	
	As quarters.	As kitchen.	As office.	From May 1 to Sept. 30.	From Oct. 1 to April 30.
A Major-General	5	1	...	1[†]	5
A Brigadier-General or Colonel	4	1	...	1	4
A Lieutenant-Colonel or Major	3	1	...	1	3½
A Captain or Chaplain	2	1	...	¾	3
Lieutenant	1	1	...	½	2
Military store-keeper	1	1	...		...
The General commanding the army	...	...	3	...	3
The commanding officer of a division or department, an assistant or deputy Quartermaster-General	...	...	2	...	2
The commanding officer of a regiment or post, Quartermaster, Assistant-Quartermaster, or Commissary of Subsistence	...	...	1	...	1
The senior Ordnance Officer stationed at the Head-Quarters of a Military Department	...	...	1	...	1
The Assistant Adjutant-General at the Head-Quarters of the Army, the Assistant Adjutant-General, the Medical Director and Medical Purveyor of a Military Department, each	...	...	1	...	1
Officers of the Pay Department	...	...	1	...	1
An acting Assistant-Quartermaster, when approved by the Quartermaster-General	...	...	1	...	1
Wagon and forage master, Sergeant-Major, Ordnance Sergeant, Quartermaster-Sergeant, Medical Cadet, or Principal Musician	1	...	...	½	1
Each non-commissioned officer, musician, private, officer's servant, and washerwoman	...	...	...	1/12	1/6
Each necessary fire for the sick in hospital, to be regulated by the surgeon and commanding officer, *not exceeding*	...	...	...	½	2
Each guard-fire, to be regulated by the commanding officer, not exceeding	...	...	...	...	3
A commissary or quartermaster's store-house, when necessary, *not exceeding*	...	...	...	...	1
A regiment or post mess	1	...	...	...	1
To every six non-commissioned officers, musicians, and privates, servants and washerwomen, 225 square feet of room north of 38° N., and 256 square feet south of that latitude.					

[*]Or coal, at the rate of 1500 lbs. anthracite, or 30 bushels bituminous, to the cord.
[†]Two cords of pine wood for fuel may, at the discretion of a department commander be issued in lieu of one cord of oak, provided the cost be not greater.

1069. Merchantable hard wood is the standard; the cord is 128 cubic feet.

1070. A particular set of quarters will be set apart at every chaplain post for the chaplain. He will not be disturbed in these further than by a reduction of his allowance when that of the other officers is reduced Nor will he be alloyed to choose other quarters.

1071. No officer shall occupy more than his proper quarters, except by order of the commanding officer when there is an excess of quarters at the station; which order the quartermaster shall forward to the Quartermaster-General, to be laid before the Secretary of War. But the amount of quarters shall be reduced *pro rata* by the commanding officer when the number of officers and troops make it necessary; and when the public buildings are not sufficient to quarter the troops, the commanding officer shall report to the commander of the department for authority to hire quarters, or other necessary orders in the case. The department commander shall report the case, and his orders therein, to the Quartermaster-General.

1072. A mess-room, and fuel for it, are allowed only when a majority of the officers of a post or regiment unite in a mess; never to less than three officers, nor to any who live in hotels or boarding-houses. Fuel for a mess-room shall not be used elsewhere, or for any other purpose.

1073. Fuel issued to officers or troops is public property for their use; what they do not actually consume shall be returned to the quartermaster and taken up on his quarterly return. With this exception, however: that the fuel issued to troops, and not actually used in quarters, may be used in baking their bread.

1074. In November, December, January, and February, the fuel is increased one-fourth at stations from the 39th degree to the 43d degree north latitude, and one-third at stations north of the 43d degree.

1075. Fuel shall be issued only in the month when due.

1076. In allotting quarters, officers shall have choice according to rank, but the commanding officer may direct the officers to be stationed convenient to their troops.

1077. An officer may select quarters occupied by a junior; but, having made his choice, he must abide by it, and shall not again at the post displace a junior, unless himself displaced by a senior.

1078. The set of rooms to each quarters will be assigned by the quartermaster, under the control of the commanding officer; attics not counted as rooms.

1079. Officers cannot choose rooms in different sets of quarters.

1080. When public quarters cannot be furnished to officers at stations without troops, or to enlisted men at general or department head-quarters, quarters will be commuted at a rate fixed by the Secretary of War, and fuel at the market price delivered. When fuel and quarters are commuted to an officer by reason of his employment on a civil work, the commutation shall be charged to the appropriation for the work. No commutation of rooms or fuel is allowed for offices or messes.

1081. The following rates of monthly commutation for quarters, when officers are serving without troops and at posts where there are no public quarters which they can occupy, have been established:

1. At Boston, New York, Philadelphia, Baltimore, Washington City, Charleston, Key West, Mobile, and New Orleans, and at all posts and stations in Texas, and in the Territories of New Mexico, Oregon, and Washington, $9 per room.
2. At Detroit, Chicago, and St. Louis, and at all places east of the Rocky Mountains, not heretofore enumerated, $8 per room.
3. At San Francisco, $20 per room, and at all other places in California, $12 per room.

1084. Officers and troops in the field are not entitled to commutation for quarters or fuel.

1095. Military posts evacuated by the troops, and lands reserved for military use, will be put in charge of the Quartermaster's Department, unless otherwise specially ordered.

ARMY TRANSPORTATION.

1096. When troops are moved, or officers travel with escorts or stores, the means of transport provided shall be for the whole command. Proper orders in the case, and an exact return of the command, including officers' servants and company women, will be furnished to the quartermaster who is to provide the transportation.

1097. The baggage to be transported is limited to camp and garrison equipage, and officers' baggage. Officers' baggage shall not exceed (mess chest and all personal effects included) as follows:

	In the field.	Changing stations.
General officers	125 pounds.	1000 pounds.
Field officers	100 "	800 "
Captains	80 "	700 "
Subalterns	80 "	600 "

These amounts shall be reduced *pro rata* by the commanding officer when necessary, and may be increased by the Quartermaster-General on transports by water, when proper in special cases.

1098. The regimental and company desk prescribed in army regulations will be transported; also for staff officers, the books, papers, and instruments necessary to their duties; and for medical officers, their medical chest. In doubtful cases under this regulation, and whenever baggage exceeds the regulated allowance, the conductor of the train, or officer in charge of the transportation, will report to the commanding officer, who will order an inspection, and all excess to be rejected.

1102. Where officers' horses are to be transported, it must be authorized in the orders for the movement.

1103. The baggage trains, ambulances, and all the means of transport continue in charge of the proper officers of the Quartermaster's Department, under the control of the commanding officers.

1104. In all cases of transportation, whether of troops or stores, an exact return of the amount and kind of transportation employed will be made by the quartermaster to the Quartermaster-General, accompanied by the orders for the movement, a return of the troops, and an invoice of the stores.

1105. Wagons and their equipments for the transport service of the army will be procured, when practicable, from the Ordnance Department, and fabricated in the government establishments.

1106. Spring wagons or carriages will not be used except on extraordinary occasions, and then only on the written order of a department commander or the commander of an army in the field, a copy of which order will be transmitted to the Quartermaster-General. The purchase of this description of conveyance is prohibited, unless specially authorized by the War Department.

FORAGE.

1121. The forage ration is fourteen pounds of hay and twelve pounds of oats, corn, or barley. For mules, fourteen pounds of hay and nine pounds of oats, corn, or barley.

1122. The allowance of forage to mounted officers will apply for mules equally as for horses, when the exigencies of the service make it necessary to use the former instead of the latter. This will not authorize officers to make the substitution on drills and parades, or, under ordinary circumstances, on any duty under arms.

1124. No officer shall sell forage issued to him. Forage issued to public horses or cattle is public property; what they do not actually consume is to be properly accounted for.

STRAW.

1126. In barracks, twelve pounds of straw per month for bedding will be allowed to each man, servant, and company woman.

1127. The allowance and change of straw for the sick is regulated by the surgeon.

1128. One hundred pounds per month allowed for bedding to each horse in public service.

1129. At posts near prairie land owned by the United States, hay will be used instead of straw, and provided by the troops. Straw not actually used as bedding shall be accounted for as other public property.

STATIONERY.

1131. When an officer is relieved in command, he shall transfer the office stationery to his successor.

1132. To each office table is allowed one inkstand, one stamp, one paper-folder, one sand-box, one wafer-box, and as many lead-pencils as may be required, not exceeding four per annum.

1133. Necessary stationery for military courts and boards will be furnished on the requisition of the recorder, approved by the presiding officer.

1135. Regimental, company, and post books, and printed blanks for the officers of Quartermaster and Pay Departments, will be procured by timely requisition on the Quartermaster-General.

1136. Printed matter procured by the Quartermaster-General for use out of Washington may be procured elsewhere, at a cost not to exceed the rates prescribed by Congress for the public printing increased by the cost of transportation.

EXPENSES OF COURTS-MARTIAL.

1137. An officer who attends a general court-martial or court of inquiry, convened by authority competent to order a general court-martial, will be paid, if the court is not held at the station where he is at the time serving, one dollar a day while attending the court and traveling to and from it if entitled to forage, and one dollar and twenty-five cents a day if not entitled to forage.

1138. The Judge Advocate or Recorder will be paid, besides, a per diem of one dollar and twenty-five, cents for every day he is necessarily employed in the duty of the court. When it is necessary to employ a clerk to aid the Judge Advocate, the court may order it; a soldier to be procured when practicable.

1139. A citizen witness shall be paid his actual transportation or stage fare, and three dollars a day while attending the court and traveling to and from it, counting the travel at fifty miles a day.

EXTRA-DUTY MEN.

1141. Duplicate rolls of the extra-duty men, to be paid by the Quartermaster's Department, will be made monthly, and certified by the quartermaster, or other officer having charge of the work, and countersigned by the commanding officer. One of these will be transmitted direct to the Quartermaster-General, and the other filed in support of the pay-roll.

PUBLIC POSTAGE.

1142. Postage and dispatches by telegraph, on public business, paid by an officer, will be refunded to him on his certificate to the account, and to the necessity of the communication by telegraph. The amount for postage, and for telegraph dispatches, will be stated separately. The telegraph should be used only in cases of urgent and imperative necessity, where the delay of the mail would be prejudicial to the public interest. Copies of the telegrams must accompany vouchers for their payment.

HORSES FOR MOUNTED OFFICERS.

1143. In the field, on the frontier, or in active service, the commanding officer may authorize a mounted officer to take from the public stables one or two horses at a price one-third greater than the average cost of the lot from which he selects, or at the actual cost of the horse when that can be ascertained; providing he shall not take the horse of any trooper. A horse so taken shall not be exchanged or returned. Horses of mounted officers shall be shod by the public farrier or blacksmith.

1144. The horses of a field battery will be shod by the artificers of the company, one of whom shall be a farrier. No other compensation than the pay and allowances of that grade will be made for these services.

CLOTHING, CAMP AND GARRISON EQUIPAGE.

1145. Supplies of clothing and camp and garrison equipage will be sent by the Quartermaster-General from the general depôt to the officers of his department stationed with the troops.

1149. Bed-sacks are provided for troops in garrison, and iron pots may be furnished to them instead of camp-kettles. Requisitions will be sent to the Quartermaster-General for the authorized flags, colors, standards, guidons, drums, fifes, bugles, and trumpets.

ALLOWANCE OF CLOTHING.

1150. A soldier is allowed the uniform clothing stated in the following table, or articles thereof of equal value. When a balance is due him at the end of a year, it is added to his allowance for the next.

CLOTHING.	FOR FIVE YEARS.					Total in the five years.
	1st.	2d.	3d.	4th.	5th.	
Cap, complete	2	1	2	1	1	7
Hat with trimmings complete	1	1	1	1	1	5
Fatigue forage caps, of pattern in the Quartermaster-General's Office, will be issued, in addition to hats	1	1	1	1	1	5
Pompon	1	...	1	...	...	2
Eagle and ring	1	...	1	...	...	2
Cover	1	1	1	1	1	5
Coat	2	1	2	1	2	8
Trowsers	3	2	3	2	3	13
Flannel shirt	3	3	3	3	3	15
" drawers	3	2	2	2	2	11
Bootees,* pair	4	4	4	4	4	20
Stockings, pair	4	4	4	4	4	20
Leather stock	1	...	1	...	...	2
Great-coat	1	...	...	...	...	1
Stable-frock (for mounted men)	1	...	1	...	...	2
Fatigue overalls (for engineers and ordnance)	1	1	1	1	1	5
Blanket	1	...	1	...	...	2

*Mounted men may receive *one* pair of "boots" and *two* pairs of "bootees" instead of *four* pairs of bootees.

1151. One sash is allowed to each company for the first sergeant, and one knapsack with straps, haversack, and canteen with straps, to each enlisted man. These and the metallic scales, letters, numbers, castles, shells, and flames, and the camp and garrison equipage, will not be returned as issued, but borne on the return while fit for service. They will be charged to the person in whose use they are, when lost or destroyed by his fault.

1152. Commanders of companies draw the clothing of their men, and the camp and garrison equipage for the officers and men of their company. The camp and garrison equipage of other officers is drawn on their own receipts.

1153. When clothing is needed for issue to the men, the company commander will procure it from the quartermaster on requisition, approved by the commanding officer.

1154. Ordinarily the company commander will procure and issue clothing to his men twice a year; at other times, when necessary in special cases.

1155. Such articles of clothing as the soldier may need will be issued to him. When the issues equal in value his allowance for the year, further issues are extra issues, to be charged to him on the next muster-roll.

1156. The talmas furnished the mounted troops will be accounted for as company property, and the men to whom they are issued will be held responsible for their preservation.

1157. The money value of the clothing, and of each article of it, will be ascertained annually, and announced in orders from the War Department.

1158. Officers receiving clothing, or camp and garrison equipage, will render quarterly returns of it to the Quartermaster-General.

1165. Commanding officers may order necessary issues of clothing to prisoners and convicts, taking deserters' or other damaged clothing when there is such in store.

1166. Officers of the army may purchase, at the regulation price, from the quartermaster of their post, such articles of uniform clothing as they actually need—certifying that the articles so drawn are intended solely for their own personal use.

1167. But—with the exception of under-clothing and shoes, of which, when there are no other means of procuring them, a reasonable quantity may, on the officers' certificate to that effect, be purchased for them from the quartermaster—no officer's private servant, not a soldier, shall be permitted to draw or to wear the uniform clothing issued to the troops.

1175. Officers serving in the Quartermaster's Department will report to the Quartermaster-General useful information in regard to the routes and means of transportation and of supplies.

ARTICLE XLIII.

SUBSISTENCE DEPARTMENT.

1176. The Commissary-General of Subsistence will designate, as far as practicable, the places where contracts and purchases for subsistence supplies shall be made, and, under the direction of the Secretary of War, assign to stations and duties the officers and agents of his Department.

SUBSISTENCE SUPPLIES.

1177. These supplies comprise: 1st, articles composing the ration, such as pork, flour, coffee, candles, &c., called SUBSISTENCE STORES; 2d, the necessary means of issuing and preserving these stores, such as stationery, scales, measures, tools, &c., called COMMISSARY PROPERTY. Subsistence supplies shall not be transferred gratuitously to another staff-department, nor obtained, issued, sold, or otherwise disposed of, except as herein prescribed.

CONTRACTS.[*]

1179. Contracts for subsistence stores shall be made after due public notice, and on the lowest proposal received from a responsible person who produces the required article. These agreements shall expressly provide for their termination at such times as the Commissary-General may direct, and for the exclusion of any interest in them on the part of members of Congress, officers or agents of the Government, and all persons employed in the public service. (Forms 36 and 37.)

PURCHASES.

1186. Subsistence supplies purchased by a Commissary, or agent, whether paid for or not, must be accounted for by him on the proper Return. (Forms 1 and 8.) The *name* of each person from whom stores have been purchased during a month, *date* of purchase, *articles* and *quantities* procured, must be entered *on the Return of Provisions* for that month (Form 1), or, when the purchase bills are many, *on the Abstract* which accompanies the Return. (Form 6.) When stores are purchased but not paid for, a note to that effect will be entered by the purchasing officer or agent, in the column of "Remarks" to his Return of Provisions, or its accompanying Abstract.

STORAGE.

1189. Good and sufficient storehouses, sheds, paulins, or other proper and adequate means of covering and protecting subsistence supplies, will be provided by the Quartermaster's Department. Care must be taken to keep the store-rooms dry and well ventilated.

---

[*]See Act, approved July 17, 1862.

THE RATION.*

1190. A ration is the established daily allowance of food for one person. For the United States army it is composed as follows: twelve ounces of pork or bacon, or, one pound and four ounces of salt or fresh beef; one pound and six ounces of soft bread or flour, or, one pound of hard bread, or, one pound and four ounces of corn meal; and to every one hundred rations, fifteen pounds of beans or peas,[†] *and* ten pounds of rice or hominy; ten pounds of green coffee, or, eight pounds of roasted (or roasted and ground) coffee, or, one pound and eight ounces of tea; fifteen pounds of sugar; four quarts of vinegar; one pound and four ounces of adamantine or star candles; four pounds of soap; three pounds and twelve ounces of salt;[†] four ounces of pepper; thirty pounds of potatoes,[†] when practicable, and one quart of molasses. The Subsistence Department, as may be most convenient or least expensive to it, and according to the condition and amount of its supplies, shall determine whether soft bread or flour, and what other component parts of the ration, as equivalents, shall be issued.

1191. Desiccated compressed potatoes, or desiccated compressed mixed vegetables, at the rate of one ounce and a half of the former, and one ounce of the latter, to the ration, may be *substituted* for beans, peas, rice, hominy, or fresh potatoes.

1192. Sergeants and corporals of the Ordnance Department (heretofore classed as armorers, carriage-makers, and blacksmiths) are entitled, each, to one and a half rations per day; all other enlisted men, to one ration a day.

---

*"After the present insurrection shall cease, the ration shall be as provided by law and regulations on the first day of July, eighteen hundred and sixty-one." (Section 13, Act approved August 3, 1861.)

†Beans, peas, salt, and potatoes (fresh) shall be purchased, issued, and sold by weight, and the *bushel* of each shall be estimated at *sixty pounds.* Thus, 100 rations of beans or peas will be fifteen pounds, the equivalent of eight quarts; 100 rations of salt will be three pounds and twelve ounces, the equivalent of two quarts; and 100 rations of potatoes (fresh) will be thirty pounds, the equivalent of half a bushel.

ISSUES IN BULK.

1194. Stores longest on hand shall be issued first, whether the issue be in bulk or on ration returns.

1196. Any deficiency of supplies not attributable to ordinary loss in transportation, any damage, or discrepancy between the invoices and actual quantity or description of supplies received, shall be investigated by a board of survey. . . . The officer revising the action of the board shall immediately transmit a copy of its proceedings to the Commissary-General of Subsistence, and a copy to the issuing Commissary. A copy of the proceedings of the board shall also accompany the receiving Commissary's Return of Provisions to the Commissary-General of Subsistence. Where the carrier is liable, the issuing Commissary shall report the amount of loss or damage to the Quartermaster authorized to pay the transportation account, in order that this amount may be recovered for the Subsistence Department.

ISSUES TO TROOPS.

1198. Subsistence shall be issued to troops on ration returns signed by their immediate commander, and approved by the commanding officer of the post or station. . . .

ISSUES TO CITIZENS.

1201. One ration a day may be issued to each person employed with the army, when such are the terms of his engagement, on returns similar to Form 13. No hired person shall draw more than one ration per day.

ISSUES TO INDIANS.

1202. When subsistence can be spared from the military supplies, the commanding officer is authorized to allow its issue, *in small quantities*, to Indians visiting military posts on the frontiers or in their respective nations. The return for this issue shall be signed by the Indian agent (when there is one present), and approved by the commanding officer of the post or station.

1203. Regular daily or periodical issues of subsistence to Indians, or issues of subsistence *in bulk* to Indian agents for the use of Indians, are forbidden.

ISSUES EXTRA.

1205. Extra issues will be allowed as follows, viz.:

WHISKY.

One gill per man daily, in cases of *excessive* fatigue, or *severe* exposure. The *number* of men issued to will be stated on each return for extra issues, and so entered on the Abstract. Under "Remarks," on the return and on the Abstract, the letters of companies to which the men belong, *number* and designation of regiment, &c., will be given.

BEEF CATTLE.

1220. When practicable, beef cattle presented for acceptance, whether procured under contract or purchased in open market, must be weighed on the scales. From the live weight of a steer thus ascertained, his net weight shall be determined by deducting forty-five per cent, when his gross weight exceeds thirteen hundred (1300) pounds, and fifty per cent, when less than that, and not under eight hundred (800) pounds. When it is impracticable to weigh on the scales, one or more *average* steers must be selected, killed, and dressed in the usual manner. The average net weight of these (necks, shanks, and kidney tallow excluded) shall be accepted as the average net weight of the herd.

1221. In all written instruments for the delivery of beef cattle, the manner prescribed above for determining net weight must be inserted; in verbal agreements (which will be allowed only when time does not admit of reducing to writing the terms agreed upon) this mode must be understood and accepted by the party delivering the cattle.

1222. Hay, corn, and other forage will be procured for beef cattle when the pasture is insufficient.

1223. Beef received on the hoof, whether under contract, by open purchase, or otherwise, shall be accounted for on the Return of Provisions by the *number* of cattle, and by their *net* weight in pounds. When beef cattle are transferred, they should be appraised, if possible, and their loss or gain in weight since previous appraisement reported by the officer delivering the cattle.

ARTICLE XLIV.

MEDICAL DEPARTMENT.

1266. The medical supplies for the army are prescribed in the standard supply tables.

1267. The medical purveyors and the senior medical officer of each hospital, post, or command, will make the necessary requisitions for medical and hospital supplies, in duplicate (Form 1). If the supplies are to be obtained from the principal purveying depôts, the requisitions will be made upon the Surgeon-General on the 31st day of December annually; if from department or field depôts, they will be made upon the medical director at such times and for such periods as he may direct. Good vaccine matter will be kept on hand by timely requisition on the Surgeon-General.

1284. At surgeon's call the sick then in the companies will be conducted to the hospital by the first sergeants, who will each hand to the surgeon, in his company book, a list of all the sick of the company, on which the surgeon shall state who are to remain or go into hospital; who are to return to quarters as sick or convalescent; what duties the convalescents in quarters are capable of; what cases are feigned; and any other information in regard to the sick of the company he may have to communicate to the company commander.

1285. Soldiers in hospital, patients, or attendants, except stewards, shall be mustered on the rolls of their company, if it be present at the post.

1287. Patients in hospital are, if possible, to leave their arms and accoutrements with their companies, and in no case to take ammunition into the hospital.

1293. The senior medical officer will select the cooks, nurses, and matrons (and, at posts where there is no hospital steward appointed by the Secretary of War, a soldier to act as steward), with the approval of the commanding officer. Cooks and nurses will be taken from the privates, and will be exempt from other duty, but shall attend the parades for muster and weekly inspections of their companies at the post, unless specially excused by the commanding officer.

1297. In passing a recruit the medical officer is to examine him stripped; to see that he has free use of all his limbs; that his chest is ample; that his hearing, vision, and speech are perfect; that he has no tumors, or ulcerated or extensively cicatrized legs; no rupture or chronic cutaneous affection; that he has not received any contusion, or wound of the head, that may impair his faculties; that he is not a drunkard; is not subject to convulsions; and has no infectious disorder, nor any other that may unfit him for military service.

1299. As soon as a recruit joins any regiment or station, he shall be examined by the medical officer, and vaccinated when it is required.

1309. When medical attendance is required by officers or enlisted men on service, or for the authorized servants of such officers, and the attendance of a medical officer cannot be had, the officer, or, if there be no officer, then the enlisted man, may employ a private physician, and a just account therefor will be paid by the medical bureau.

1317. The Secretary of War will designate the applicants to be examined for appointment of assistant surgeon. They must be between 21 and 28 years of age. The board will report their respective merits in the several branches of the examination, and their relative merit from the whole; agreeably whereto, if vacancies happen within two years thereafter, they will receive appointments and take rank in the medical corps.

1323. The Secretary of War will appoint from the enlisted men of the army, or cause to be enlisted, as many competent hospital stewards as the service may require, not to exceed one for each post.

AMBULANCES.

1329. The following amount and kind of transportation for the sick and wounded may be provided for troops on marches and in campaigns against Indians:

1. For commands of less than five companies, to each company, one two-wheeled ambulance.
2. For a battalion, of five companies, one four-wheeled and five two-wheeled ambulances.
3. For a regiment, two four-wheeled and ten two-wheeled ambulances.

1330. The following schedule of transports for the sick and wounded and for hospital supplies will be adopted for a state of war with a civilized enemy:

1. For commands of less than three companies, one two-wheeled transport cart for hospital supplies, and to each company one two-wheeled ambulance.
2. For commands of more than three and less than five companies, two two-wheeled transport carts, and to each company one two-wheeled ambulance.
3. For a battalion of five companies, one four-wheeled ambulance, five two-wheeled ambulances, and two two-wheeled transport carts. For each additional company less than ten, one two-wheeled transport cart.

4. For a regiment of ten companies, two four-wheeled ambulances, ten two-wheeled ambulances, and four two-wheeled transport carts; and for greater commands in proportion.

1331. Ambulances will not be used for any other than the specific purpose for which they are designed, viz.: the transportation of the sick and wounded; and those hereafter provided for the army, will be made according to a pattern to be furnished the Quartermaster's Department by the Surgeon-General.

1332. The transport carts must be made after the models of the two-wheeled ambulances (their interior arrangement for the sick excepted), and to have solid board flooring to the body.

1333. Horse-litters may be prepared and furnished to posts whence they may be required for service on ground not admitting the employment of two-wheeled carriages; said litters to be composed of a canvas bed similar to the present stretcher, and of two poles each sixteen feet long, to be made in sections, with head and foot pieces constructed to act as stretchers to keep the poles apart.

1334. The allowance of hospital attendants in the field will be, for one company, one steward, one nurse, and one cook; for each additional company, one nurse; and for commands of over five companies, one additional cook.

HOSPITAL TENTS.

1335. Hospital tents must in future be made according to the pattern of the present tent and of the same material, but smaller, and having on one end a lapel so as to admit of two or more tents being joined and thrown into one with a continuous covering or roof. The dimensions to be these: In length, 14 feet; in width, 15 feet; in height (centre), 11 feet, with a wall $4\frac{1}{2}$ feet, and a "fly" of appropriate size. The ridge-pole to be made in two sections after the present pattern; and to measure 14 feet when joined. Such a tent will accommodate from 8 to 10 patients comfortably.

ARTICLE XLV.

PAY DEPARTMENT.

1338. The troops will be paid in such manner that the arrears shall at no time exceed two months, unless the circumstances of the case render it unavoidable, which the paymaster charged with the payment shall promptly report to the Paymaster-General.

1339. The Paymaster-General shall take care, by timely remittances, that the paymasters have the necessary funds to pay the troops, and shall notify the remittances to the paymasters and commanding officers of the respective pay districts.

1340. The payments, except to officers and discharged soldiers, shall be made on muster and pay rolls; those of companies and detachments, signed by the company or detachment commander; of the hospital, signed by the surgeon; and all muster and pay rolls, signed by the mustering and inspecting officer.

1341. When a company is paraded for payment, the officer in command of it shall attend at the pay-table.

1345. No officer shall receive pay for two staff appointments for the same time.

1346. Officers are entitled to pay from the date of the acceptance of their appointments, and from the date of promotion.

1386. Paymasters will afford Sutlers every facility in the collection of the amounts due them in accordance with regulations 217 and 218.

1387. Officers absent from their appropriate duties, either with or without leave, for six months, will thereby forfeit all the emoluments and allowances to which they would otherwise be entitled.

ARTICLE XLVI.

CORPS OF ENGINEERS.

ARTICLE XLVI. (*pages* 379 *to* 395, *par.* 1388 *to* 1405) *contains the* REGULATIONS OF THE CORPS OF ENGINEERS, *which is published in pamphlet form, and distributed to those officers who require it, by the* CHIEF ENGINEER.

ARTICLE XLVII.

ORDNANCE DEPARTMENT.

1406. The Ordnance Department has charge of the arsenals and armories, and furnishes all ordnance and ordnance stores for the military service.

1407. The general denomination, "Ordnance and Ordnance Stores," comprehends all cannon and artillery carriages and equipments; all apparatus and machines for the service and manœuvres of artillery; all small arms and accoutrements and horse equipments; all ammunition; all tools and materials for the ordnance service; horse medicines, materials for shoeing, and all horse equipments whatever for the light artillery.

1408. Models or patterns proposed by the Ordnance Board and approved by the Secretary of War, of all ordnance and ordnance stores for the land service of the United States, with the standard gauges, weights, and measures, shall be deposited in the model office at the Washington arsenal; and no change or variation from them shall be allowed, except on the recommendation of the board, approved by the Secretary of War. The ordnance board is composed of such officers of that department as the Secretary of War may designate.

1410. The purchases and contracts for cannon, projectiles, powder, small arms, and accoutrements are made, or specially ordered by the chief of ordnance, under the direction of the Secretary of War.

1419. When arms, accoutrements, and equipments need repairs that cannot be made by the troops, the commanding officer may send them to be repaired to the most convenient arsenal.

1420. The commander of each company or detachment will be accountable for all ordnance and ordnance stores issued to his command. The commander of each post will be accountable for all ordnance and ordnance stores at the post, not issued to the company or detachment commanders, or not in charge of an officer of ordnance or a store-keeper. Ordnance sergeants will account for ordnance property only where there is no commissioned officer of the army or store-keeper.

1422. Enlisted men who lose, or dispose of, the Colt's revolver pistols intrusted to their care, will hereafter be charged forty dollars in each case; that owing the amount of pecuniary damage sustained by the United States, as estimated by the Ordnance Department.

1443. No trees on the public grounds will be removed or destroyed without authority from the ordnance bureau.

1444. None but strong draft horses are to be purchased for the ordnance service, nor without authority from the chief of ordnance.

1445. The enlisted men of ordnance shall be enlisted in the grade of laborer. They may be mustered, at the discretion of the officer in command, in any grade for which they are competent, except the grade of master workman. Promotions to that grade require the sanction of the chief of ordnance. Enlistments (Form 24) are to be in duplicate; one filed at the post, the other forwarded to the ordnance bureau. The number of enlisted men at each arsenal will be directed by the chief of ordnance.

ARTICLE XLVIII.

PROCEEDINGS IN CIVIL COURTS.

1461. When an officer is made a party to any action or proceeding in a civil court which may involve the interest of the

United States; or when, by the performance of his public duty, he is involved in any action or proceeding in which he claims protection or indemnity from the United States, he shall promptly report the case to the Adjutant-General, to be laid before the Secretary of War.

1462. In ordinary cases, when an officer is called upon to show by what authority he holds a soldier in service, he can himself set forth the facts, and need not employ counsel. In important cases, if counsel be necessary, and there is not time to obtain the previous authority of the War Department, he will forthwith report the facts to the Adjutant-General.

ARTICLE XLIX.

ARMS OF THE UNITED STATES.

1463. *Arms*—Paleways of thirteen pieces, argent and gules; a chief, azure; the escutcheon on the breast of the American eagle displayed, proper, holding in his dexter talon an olive-branch, and in his sinister a bundle of thirteen arrows, all proper; and in his beak a scroll, inscribed with this motto: "E PLURIBUS UNUM."

For the *crest*: over the head of the eagle, which appears above the escutcheon, a glory breaking through a cloud, proper, and surrounding thirteen stars, forming a constellation, argent, and on an azure field.

ARTICLE L.

FLAGS, COLORS, STANDARDS, GUIDONS.

GARRISON FLAG.

1464. The garrison flag is the national flag. It is made of bunting, thirty-six feet fly, and twenty feet hoist, in thirteen horizontal stripes of equal breadth, alternately red and white, beginning with the red. In the upper quarter, next the staff, is the Union, composed of a number of white stars, equal to the number of States, on a blue field, one-third the length of the flag, extend-

ing to the lower edge of the fourth red stripe from the top. The storm flag is twenty feet by ten feet; the recruiting flag, nine feet nine inches by four feet four inches.

COLORS OF ARTILLERY REGIMENTS.

1465. Each regiment of Artillery shall have two silken colors. The first, or the national color, of stars and stripes, as described for the garrison flag. The number and name of the regiment to be embroidered with gold on the centre stripe. The second, or regimental color, to be yellow, of the same dimensions as the first, bearing in the centre two cannon crossing, with the letters U. S. above, and the number of the regiment below; fringe, yellow. Each color to be six feet six inches fly, and six feet deep on the pike. The pike, including the spear and ferrule, to be nine feet ten inches in length. Cords and tassels, red and yellow silk intermixed.

COLORS OF INFANTRY REGIMENTS.

1466. Each regiment of Infantry shall have two silken colors. The first, or the national color, of stars and stripes, as described for the garrison flag; the number and name of the regiment to be embroidered with silver on the centre stripe. The second, or regimental color, to be blue, with the arms of the United States embroidered in silk on the centre. The name of the regiment in a scroll, underneath the eagle. The size of each color to be six feet six inches fly, and six feet deep on the pike. The length of the pike, including the spear and ferrule, to be nine feet ten inches. The fringe yellow; cords and tassels, blue and white silk intermixed.

CAMP COLORS.

1467. The camp colors are of bunting, eighteen inches square; white for infantry, and red for artillery, with the number of the regiment on them. The pole eight feet long.

STANDARDS AND GUIDONS OF MOUNTED REGIMENTS.

1468. Each regiment will have a silken standard, and each company a silken guidon. The standard to bear the arms of the United States, embroidered in silk, on a blue ground, with the number and name of the regiment, in a scroll underneath the eagle. The flag of the standard to be two feet five inches wide, and two feet three inches on the lance, and to be edged with yellow silk fringe.

1469. The flag of the guidon is swallow-tailed, three feet five inches from the lance to the end of the swallow-tail; fifteen inches to the fork of the swallow-tail, and two feet three inches on the lance. To be half red and half white, dividing at the fork, the red above. On the red, the letters U. S. in white; and on the white, the letter of the company in red. The lance of the standards and guidons to be nine feet long, including spear and ferrule.

ARTICLE LI.

UNIFORM, DRESS, AND HORSE EQUIPMENTS.

COAT.

For Commissioned Officers.

1470. All officers shall wear a frock-coat of dark blue cloth, the skirt to extend from two-thirds to three-fourths of the distance from the top of the hip to the bend of the knee; single-breasted for Captains and Lieutenants; double-breasted for all other grades.

1471. *For a Major-General*—two rows of buttons on the breast, nine in each row, placed by threes; the distance between each row, five and one-half inches at top, and three and one-half inches at bottom; stand-up collar, to rise no higher than to permit the chin to turn freely over it, to hook in front at the bottom, and slope thence up and backward at an angle of thirty degrees on each side; cuffs two and one-half inches deep to go around the sleeves parallel with the lower edge, and to button with three small buttons at the under seam; pockets in the folds of the skirts, with one button at the hip, and one at the end of each pocket, making four buttons on the back and skirt of the coat, the hip button to range with the lowest buttons on the breast; collar and cuffs to be of dark blue velvet; lining of the coat black.

1472. *For a Brigadier-General*—the same for a Major-General, except that there will be only eight buttons in each row on the breast, placed in pairs.

1473. *For a Colonel*—the same as for a Major-General, except that there will be only seven buttons in each row on the breast, placed at equal distances; collar and cuffs of the same color and material as the coat.

1474. *For a Lieutenant-Colonel*—the same as for a Colonel.

1475. *For a Major*—the same as for a Colonel.

1476. *For a Captain*—the same as for a Colonel, except that there will be only one row of nine buttons on the breasts, placed at equal distances.

1477. *For a First Lieutenant*—the same as for a Captain.

1478. *For a Second Lieutenant*—the same as for a Captain.

1479. *For a Brevet Second Lieutenant*—the same as for a Captain.

1480. *For a Medical Cadet*—the same as for a Brevet Second Lieutenant.

1481. A round jacket, according to pattern, of dark blue cloth, trimmed with scarlet, with the Russian shoulder-knot, the prescribed insignia of rank to be worked in silver in the centre of the knot, may be worn on undress duty by officers of Light Artillery.

For Enlisted Men

1482. The uniform coat for all enlisted *foot* men, shall be a single-breasted frock of dark blue cloth, made without plaits, with a skirt extending one-half the distance from the top of the hip to the bend of the knee; one row of nine buttons on the breast, placed at equal distances; stand-up collar to rise no higher than to permit the chin to turn freely over it, to hook in front at the bottom and then to slope up and backward at an angle of thirty degrees on each side; cuffs pointed according to pattern, and to button with two small buttons at the under seam; collar and cuffs edged with a cord or welt of cloth as follows, to wit: Scarlet *for Artillery*; sky-blue *for Infantry*; yellow *for Engineers*; crimson *for Ordnance* and *Hospital stewards*. On each shoulder a metallic scale according to pattern; narrow lining for skirt of the coat of the same color and material as the coat; pockets in the folds of the skirts with one button at each hip to range with the lowest buttons on the breast; no buttons at the ends of the pockets.

1483. *All Enlisted Men of the Cavalry and Light Artillery* shall wear a uniform jacket of dark blue cloth, with one row of twelve small buttons on the breast placed at equal distances; stand-up collar to rise no higher than to permit the chin to turn freely over it, to hook in front at the bottom, and to slope the same as the coat-collar; on the collar, on each side, two blind button-holes of lace, three-eighths of an inch wide, one small button on the button-hole, lower button-hole extending back four inches, upper button-hole three and a half inches; top button and front ends of collar bound with lace three-eighths of an inch wide, and a strip of the same extending down the front and around the whole lower edge of the jacket; the back seam laced with the same, and on the cuff a point of the same shape as that on the coat, but formed of the lace; jacket to extend to the waist, and to be lined with white flannel; two small buttons at the under seam of the cuff, as on the coat cuff; one hook and eye at the bottom of the collar; color of lace (worsted), yellow for *Cavalry*, and scarlet for *Light Artillery*.

1484. *For all Musicians*—the same as for other enlisted men of their respective corps, with the addition of a facing of lace three-eighths of an inch wide on the front of the *coat or jacket*, made in the following manner: bars of three-eighths of an inch worsted lace placed on a line with each button six and one-half inches wide at the bottom, and thence gradually expanding upward to the last button, counting from the waist up, and contracting from thence to the bottom of the collar, where it will be six and one-half inches wide, with a strip of the same lace following the bars at their outer extremity—the whole presenting something of what is called the herring-bone form; the color of the lace facing to correspond with the color of the trimming of the corps.

1485. *For Fatigue Purposes*—a sack coat of dark blue flannel extending half-way down the thigh, and made loose, without sleeve or body lining, falling collar, inside pocket on the left side, four coat buttons down the front.

1486. *For Recruits*—the sack coat will be made with sleeves and body lining, the latter of flannel.

1487. On all occasions of duty, except fatigue, and when out of quarters, the coat or jacket shall be buttoned and hooked at the collar.

BUTTONS.

1488. *For General Officers and Officers of the General Staff*—gilt, convex, with spread eagle and stars, and plain border; large size, seven-eighths of an inch in exterior diameter; small size, one-half inch.

1489. *For Officers of the Corps of Engineers*—gilt, nine-tenths of an inch in exterior diameter, slightly convex; a raised bright rim, one-thirtieth of an inch wide; device, an eagle holding in his beak a scroll, with the word, *"Essayons,"* a bastion with embrasures in the distance surrounded by water, with a rising sun—the figures to be of dead gold upon a bright field. Small buttons of the same form and device, and fifty-five hundredths of an inch in exterior diameter.

1490. *For Officers of the Corps of Topographical Engineers*—gilt, seven-eighths of an inch exterior diameter, convex and solid; device, the shield of the United States, occupying one-half the diameter, and the letters 𝔗. 𝔈. in old English characters; the other half small buttons, one-half inch diameter, device and form the same.

1491. *For Officers of the Ordnance Department*—gilt, convex, plain border, cross cannon and bombshell, with a circular scroll over and across the cannon, containing the words "Ordnance Corps;" large size, seven-eighths of an inch in exterior diameter; small size, one-half inch.

1492. *For Officers of Artillery, Infantry, and Cavalry*—gilt, convex; device, a spread eagle with the letter A, for Artillery—I, for Infantry—C, for Cavalry, on the shield; large size, seven-eighths of an inch in exterior diameter; small size, one-half inch.

1493. *Aides-de-Camp* may wear the button of the General Staff, or of their regiment or corps, at their option.

1494. *For Medical Cadets*—same as for Officers of the General Staff.

1495. *For all Enlisted Men*—yellow, the same as is used by the Artillery, &c., omitting the letter in the shield.

TROWSERS.

1496. *For General Officers and Officers of the Ordnance Department*—of dark blue cloth, plain, without stripe, welt, or cord down the outer seam.

1497. *For Officers of the General Staff and Staff Corps*, except the Ordnance—dark blue cloth, with a gold cord, one-eighth of an inch in diameter, along the outer seam.

1498. *For all Regimental Officers*—dark blue cloth, with a welt let into the outer seam, one-eighth of an inch in diameter, of colors corresponding to the facings of the respective regiments, viz.: *Cavalry*, yellow; *Artillery*, scarlet; *Infantry*, sky-blue.

1499. *For Medical Cadets*—same as for Officers of the general Staff, except a welt of buff cloth, instead of a gold cord.

1500. *For Enlisted Men*, except companies of Light Artillery—dark blue cloth; sergeants with a stripe one and one-half inch wide; *corporals* with a stripe one-half inch wide, of worsted lace, down and over the outer seam, of the color of the facings of the respective corps.

1501. *Ordnance Sergeants and Hospital Stewards*—stripe of crimson lace one and one-half inch wide.

1502. *Privates*—plain, without stripe or welt.

1503. *For Companies of Artillery equipped as Light Artillery*—sky-blue cloth. All trowsers to be made loose, without plaits, and to spread well over the boot; to be re-enforced for all enlisted mounted men.

HAT.

1504. *For Officers*—of best black felt. The dimensions of medium size to be as follows:

Width of brim, 3-$\frac{1}{4}$ inches.

Height of crown, 6-$\frac{1}{4}$ inches.

Oval of tip, $\frac{1}{2}$ inch.

Taper of crown, $\frac{3}{4}$ inch.

Curve of head, $\frac{3}{8}$ inch.

The binding to be $\frac{1}{2}$ inch deep, of best black ribbed silk.

1505. *For Enlisted Men*—of black felt, same shape and size as for officers, with double row of stitching, instead of binding, around the edge. To agree in quality with the pattern deposited in the clothing arsenal.

1506. *Medical Cadets* will wear a forage cap according to pattern.

Trimmings.

1507. *For General Officers*—gold cord, with acorn-shaped ends. The brim of the hat looped up on the right side, and fastened with an eagle attached to the side of the hat; three black ostrich-feathers; on the left side a gold-embroidered wreath in front, on black velvet ground, encircling the letters 𝕳. 𝕾. in silver, old English characters.

1508. *For Officers of the Adjutant-General's, Inspector-General's, Quartermaster's, Subsistence, Medical and Pay Departments, and the Judge Advocate, above the rank of Captain*—the same as for General Officers, except the cord, which will be of black silk and gold.

1509. *For the same Departments, below the rank of Field Officers*—the same as for Field Officers, except that there will be but two feathers.

1510. *For Officers of the Corps of Engineers*—the same as for the General Staff, except the ornament in front, which will be a gold-embroidered wreath of laurel and palm, encircling a silver turreted castle on black velvet ground.

1511. *For Officers of the Topographical Engineers*—the same as for the General Staff, except the ornament in front, which will be a gold-embroidered wreath of oak leaves, encircling a gold-embroidered shield, on black velvet ground.

1512. *For Officers of the Ordnance Department*—the same as for the General Staff, except the ornament in front, which will be a gold-embroidered shell and flame, on black velvet ground.

1513. *For Officers of Cavalry*—the same as for the General Staff, except the ornament in front, which will be two gold-embroidered sabres crossed, edges upward, on black velvet ground, with the number of the regiment in silver in the upper angle.

1514. *For Officers of Artillery*—the same as for the General Staff, except the ornament in front, which will be gold-embroidered cross-cannon, on black velvet ground, with the number of the regiment in silver at the intersection of the cross-cannon.

1515. *For Officers of Infantry*—the same as for Artillery, except the ornament in front, which will be a gold-embroidered bugle, on black velvet ground, with the number of the regiment in silver within the bend.

1516. *For Enlisted Men*, except companies of Light Artillery—the same as for officers of the respective corps, except that there will be but one feather, the cord will be of worsted, of the same color as that of the facing of the corps, three-sixteenths of an inch in diameter, running three times through a slide of the same material, and terminating with two tassels, not less than two inches long, on the side of the hat opposite the feather. The insignia of corps, in brass, in front of the hat, corresponding with those prescribed for officers, with the number of regiment, five-eighths of an inch long, in brass, and letter of company, one inch, in brass, arranged over the insignia.

1517. *For Hospital Stewards* the cord will be of buff and green mixed. The wreath in front of brass, with the letters U. S. in Roman, of white metal. Brim to be looped up to side of hat with a brass eagle, having a hook attached to the bottom to secure the brim—on the right side for mounted men and left side for foot men. The feather to be worn on the side opposite the loop.

1518. All the trimmings of the hat are to be made so that they can be detached; but the eagle, badge of corps, and letter of company, are to be always worn.

1519. For companies of Artillery equipped as Light Artillery, the old pattern uniform cap, with red horsehair plume, cord and tassel.

1520. Officers of the General Staff, and Staff Corps, may wear, at their option, a light French chapeau, either stiff crown or flat, according to the pattern deposited in the Adjutant-General's office. Officers below the rank of field officers to wear but two feathers.

FORAGE CAPS.

1521. For fatigue purposes, forage caps, of pattern in the Quartermaster-General's office: dark blue cloth, with a welt of the same around the crown, and yellow metal letters in front to designate companies.

1522. Commissioned officers may wear forage caps of the same pattern, with the distinctive ornament of the corps and regiment in front.

CRAVAT OR STOCK.

1523. *For all officers*—black; when a cravat is worn, the tie to be visible at the opening if the collar.

BOOTS.

1524. *For all Enlisted Men*—black; leather according to pattern.

1525. *For all officers*—ankle or Jefferson.

1526. *For Enlisted Men of Cavalry and Light Artillery*—ankle or Jefferson, rights and lefts, according to pattern.

1527. *For Enlisted Men of Artillery, Infantry, Engineers, and Ordnance*—Jefferson, rights and lefts, according to pattern.

SPURS.

1528. *For all Mounted Officers*—yellow metal, or gilt.

1529. *For all Enlisted Mounted Men*—yellow metal, according to pattern.

GLOVES.

1530. *For General Officers and Officers of the General Staff and Staff Corps*—buff or white.

1531. *For Officers of Artillery, Infantry, Cavalry, Dragoons, and Riflemen*—white.

SASH.

1532. *For General Officers*—buff, silk net, with silk bullion fringe ends; sash to go twice around the waist, and to tie behind the left hip, pendent part not to extend more than eighteen inches below the tie.

1533. *For Officers of the Adjutant-General's, Inspector-General's, Quartermaster's and Subsistence Departments, Corps of Engineers, Topographical Engineers, Ordnance, Artillery, Infantry, Cavalry, and the Judge Advocate of the Army*—crimson silk net; *for Officers of the Medical Department*—medium or emerald green silk net, with silk bullion fringe ends; to go around the waist and tie as for General Officers.

1534. *For all Sergeant Majors, Quartermaster Sergeants, Ordnance Sergeants, Hospital Stewards, First Sergeants, Principal or Chief Musicians and Chief Buglers*—red worsted sash, with worsted bullion fringe ends; to go twice around the waist, and to tie behind the left hip, pendent part not to extend more than eighteen inches below the tie.

1535. The sash will be worn (over the coat) on all occasions of duty of every description, except stable and fatigue.

1536. The sash will be worn by *"Officers of the Day"* across the body, scarf fashion, from the right shoulder to the left side, instead of around the waist, tying behind the left hip as prescribed.

1537. For all Officers—a waist-belt not less than one and one-half inch nor more than two inches wide; to be worn over the sash; the sword to be suspended from it by slings of the same material as the belt, with a hook attached to the belt upon which the sword may be hung.

1538. For General Officers—Russia leather, with three stripes of gold embroidery on both sides.

1539. For all other Officers—black leather, plain.

1540. For all Non-commissioned Officers—black leather, plain.

SWORD-BELT PLATE.

1541. *For all Officers and Enlisted Men*—gilt, rectangular, two inches wide, with a raised bright rim; a silver wreath of laurel encircling the "Arms of the United States;" eagle, shield, scroll, edge of cloud and ray, bright. The motto, "E PLURIBUS UNUM," in silver letters, upon the scroll; stars also of silver; according to pattern.

SWORD AND SCABBARD.

1542. *For General Officers*—straight sword, gilt hilt, silver grip, brass or steel scabbard.

1543. *For Officers of the Adjutant-General's, Inspector-General's, Quartermaster's and Subsistence Departments, Corps of Engineers, Topographical Engineers, Ordnance, the Judge Advocate of the Army, Aides-de-Camp, Field Officers of Artillery, Infantry, and Foot Riflemen, and for the Light Artillery*—the sword of the pattern adopted by the War Department, April 9, 1850; or the one described in General Orders No. 21, of August 28, 1860, for officers therein designated.

1544. *For the Medical and Pay Departments*—small sword and scabbard, according to pattern in the Surgeon-General's office.

1545. *For Medical Cadets*, the sword and belt and plate will be the same as for non-commissioned officers.

1546. *For Officers of Cavalry*—sabre and scabbard now in use, according to pattern in the Ordnance Department.

1547. *For the Artillery, Infantry, and Foot Riflemen*, except the field officers—the sword of the pattern adopted by the War Department, April 9, 1850.

1548. The sword and sword-belt will be worn upon all occasions of duty, without exception.

1549. When on foot, the sabre will be suspended from the hook attached to the belt.

1550. When not on military duty, officers may wear swords of honor, or the prescribed sword, with scabbard, gilt, or of leather with gilt mountings.

SWORD-KNOT.

1551. *For General Officers*—gold cord with acorn end.

1552. *For all other officers*—gold lace strap with gold bullion tassel.

BADGES TO DISTINGUISH RANK.

Epaulettes.

1553. *For the Major-General Commanding the Army*—gold, with solid crescent; device, three silver-embroidered stars, one, one and a half inches in diameter, one, one and one-fourth inches in diameter, and one, one and one-eighth inches in diameter, placed on the strap in a row, longitudinally, and equidistant, the largest star in the centre of the crescent, the smallest at the top; dead and bright bullion, one-half inch in diameter and three and one-half inches long.

1554. *For all other Major-Generals*—the same as for the Major-General Commanding the Army, except that there will be two stars on the strap instead of three, omitting the smallest.

1555. *For a Brigadier-General*—the same as for the Major-General, except that instead of two, there shall be one star (omitting the smallest) placed upon the strap, and not with the crescent.

1556. *For a Colonel*—the same as for a Brigadier-General, substituting a silver-embroidered spread eagle for the star upon the strap; and within the crescent for the *Medical Department*—a laurel wreath embroidered in gold, and the letters 𝔐. 𝔖., in old English characters, in silver, within the wreath; *Pay Department*—same as the Medical Department, with the letters 𝔓. 𝔇., in old English characters; *Corps of Engineers*—a turreted castle of silver; *Corps of Topographical Engineers*—a shield embroidered in gold, and below it the letters 𝔗. 𝔈., in old English characters, in silver; *Ordnance Department*—shell and flame in silver embroidery; *Regimental Officers*—the number of the regiment embroidered in gold, within a circlet of embroidered silver, one and three-fourths inches in diameter, upon cloth of the following colors: *for Artillery*—scarlet; *Infantry*—light or sky blue; *Cavalry*—yellow.

1557. *For a Lieutenant-Colonel*—the same as for a Colonel, according to corps, but substituting for the eagle a silver-embroidered leaf.

1558. *For a Major*—the same as for a Colonel, according to corps, omitting the eagle.

1559. *For a Captain*—the same as for a Colonel, according to corps, except that the bullion will be only one-fourth of an inch in diameter, and two and one-half inches long, and substituting for the eagle two silver-embroidered bars.

1560. *For a First Lieutenant*—the same as for a Colonel, according to corps, except that the bullion will be only one-eighth of an inch in diameter, and two and one-half inches long, and substituting for the eagle one silver-embroidered bar.

1561. *For a Second Lieutenant*—the same as for a First Lieutenant, omitting the bar.

1562. *For a Brevet Second Lieutenant*—the same as for a Second Lieutenant.

1563. All officers having military rank will wear an epaulette on each shoulder.

1564. The epaulette may be dispensed with when not on duty, and on certain duties off parade, to wit: at drills, at inspections of barracks and hospitals, on Courts of Inquiry and Boards, at inspections of articles and necessaries, on working parties and fatigue duties, and upon the march, except when, in war, there is immediate expectation of meeting the enemy, and also when the overcoat is worn.

Shoulder-Straps.

1565. *For the Major-General Commanding the Army*—dark blue cloth, one and three-eighths inches wide by four inches long; bordered with an embroidery of gold one-fourth of an inch wide; three silver-embroidered stars of five rays, one star on the centre of the strap, and one on each side equidistant between the centre and the outer edge of the strap; the centre star to be the largest.

1566. *For all other Major-Generals*—the same as for the Major-General Commanding the Army, except that there will be two stars on the strap instead of three, the centre of each star to be one inch from the outer edge of the gold embroidery on the ends of the strap; both stars of the same size.

1567. *For a Brigadier-General*—the same as for Major-General, except that there will be one star instead of two; the centre of the star to be equidistant from the outer edge of the embroidery on the ends of the strap.

1568. *For a Colonel*—the same size as for a Major-General, and bordered in like manner with an embroidery of gold; a silver-embroidered spread eagle on the centre of the strap, two inches between the tips of the wings, having in the right talon an olive-branch, and in the left a bundle of arrows; an escutcheon on the breast, as represented in the arms of the United States; cloth of the strap as follows: For the *General Staff and Staff Corps*—dark blue; for *Artillery*—scarlet; *Infantry*—light or sky blue; *Cavalry*—yellow.

1569. *For a Lieutenant-Colonel*—the same as for a Colonel, according to corps, but omitting the eagle, and introducing a silver-embroidered leaf at each end, each leaf extending seven-eighths of an inch from the end border of the strap.

1570. *For a Major*—the same as for a Colonel, according to corps, omitting the eagle, and introducing a gold-embroidered leaf at each end, each leaf extending seven-eighths of an inch from the end border of the strap.

1571. *For a Captain*—the same as for a Colonel, according to corps, omitting the eagle, and introducing at each end two gold-embroidered bars of the same width as the border, placed parallel to the ends of the strap; the distance between them and from the border equal to the width of the border.

1572. *For a First Lieutenant*—the same as for a Colonel, according to corps, omitting the eagle, and introducing at each end one gold-embroidered bar of the same width as the border, placed parallel to the ends of the strap, at a distance from the border equal to its width.

1573. *For a Second Lieutenant*—the same as for a Colonel, according to corps, omitting the eagle.

1574. *For a Brevet Second Lieutenant*—the same as for a Second Lieutenant.

1575. *For a Medical Cadet*—a strip of gold lace three inches long, half an inch wide, placed in the middle of a strap of green cloth three and three-quarter inches long by one and one-quarter inches wide.

1576. The shoulder-strap will be worn whenever the epaulette is not.

Chevron.

1577. The rank of non-commissioned officers will be marked by chevrons upon both sleeves of the uniform coat and overcoat, above the elbow, of silk or worsted binding one-half an inch wide, same color as the edging on the coat, points down, as follows:

1578. *For a Sergeant Major*—three bars and an arc, in silk.

1579. *For a Quartermaster Sergeant*—three bars and a tie, in silk.

1580. *For an Ordnance Sergeant*—three bars and a star, in silk.

1581. *For a Hospital Steward*—a half chevron of the following description,—viz.: of emerald green cloth, one and three-fourths inches wide, running obliquely downward from the outer to the inner seam of the sleeve, and at an angle of about thirty degrees with a horizontal, parallel to, and one-eighth of an inch distant from, both the upper and lower edge, an embroidery of yellow silk one-eighth of an inch wide, and in the centre a "caduceus" two inches long, embroidered also with yellow silk, the head toward the outer seam of the sleeve.

1582. *For a First Sergeant*—three bars and a lozenge, in worsted.

1583. *For a Sergeant*—three bars, in worsted.

1584. *For a Corporal*—two bars, in worsted.

1585. *For a Pioneer*—two crossed hatchets of cloth, same color and material as the edging of the collar, to be sewed on each arm above the elbow in the place indicated for a chevron (those of a corporal to be just above and resting on the chevron), the head of the hatchet upward, its edge outward, of the following dimensions, viz.: *Handle*—four and one-half inches long, one-fourth to one-third of an inch wide. *Hatchet*—two inches long, one inch wide at the edge.

1586. *To indicate service*—all non-commissioned officers, musicians, and privates, who have served faithfully for the term of five years, will wear, as a mark of distinction, upon both sleeves of the uniform coat, below the elbow, a diagonal half chevron, one-half an inch wide, extending from seam to seam, the front end nearest the cuff, and one-half an inch above the point of the cuff, to be of the same color as the edging on the coat. In like manner, an additional half chevron, above and parallel to the first, for every subsequent five years of faithful service; distance between each chevron one-fourth of an inch. Service in war will be indicated by a light or sky blue stripe on each side of the chevron for Artillery, and a red stripe for all other corps, the stripe to be one-eighth of an inch wide.

OVERCOAT.

For Commissioned Officers.

1587. A *"cloak coat"* of dark blue cloth, closing by means of four frog buttons of black silk and loops of black silk cord down the breast, and at the throat by a long loop *à échelle*, without tassel or plate, on the left side, and a black silk frog button on the right; cord for the loops fifteen-hundredths of an inch in diameter; back, a single piece, slit up from the bottom, from fifteen to seventeen inches, according to the height of the wearer, and closing at will, by buttons, and button-holes cut in a concealed flap; collar of the same color and material as the coat, rounded at the edges, and to stand or fall; when standing, to be about five inches high; sleeves loose, of a single piece, and round at the bottom, without cuff or slit; lining, woolen; around the front and lower border, the edges of the pockets, the edges of the sleeves, collar, and slit in the back, a flat braid of black silk one-half inch wide; and around each frog button on the breast, a knot two and one-quarter inches in diameter of black silk cord, seven-hundredths of an inch in diameter, arranged according to drawing; cape of the same color and material as the coat, removable at the pleasure of the wearer, and reaching to the cuff of the coat-sleeve when the arm is extended; coat to extend down the leg from six to eight inches below the knee, according to height. *To indicate rank*, there will be on both sleeves, near the lower edge, a knot of flat black silk braid not exceeding one-eighth of an inch in width, arranged according to drawing, and composed as follows:

1588. *For a General*—of five braids, double knot.

1589. *For a Colonel*—of five braids, single knot.

1590. *For a Lieutenant-Colonel*—of four braids, single knot.

1591. *For a Major*—of three braids, single knot.

1592. *For a Captain*—of two braids, single knot.

1593. *For a First Lieutenant*—of one braid, single knot.

1594. *For a Second Lieutenant and Brevet Second Lieutenant*—a plain sleeve, without knot or ornament.

For Enlisted Men.

1595. *Of all Mounted Corps*—of sky-blue cloth; stand-and-fall collar; double-breasted; cape to reach down to the cuff of the coat when the arm is extended, and to button all the way up; buttons (1495).

1596. *All other Enlisted Men*—of sky-blue cloth; stand-up collar; single-breasted; cape to reach down to the elbows when the arm is extended, and to button all the way up; buttons (1467).

1597. *For Cavalry*—a gutta-percha talma, or cloak extending to the knee, with long sleeves.

OTHER ARTICLES OF CLOTHING AND EQUIPMENT.

1598. *Flannel shirt, drawers, stockings, and stable-frock*—the same as now furnished.

1599. *Blanket*—woolen, gray, with letters U.S. in black, four inches long, in the centre; to be seven feet long, and five and a half feet wide, and to weigh five pounds.

1600. *Canvas overalls for Engineer soldiers*—of white cotton; one garment to cover the whole of the body below the waist, the breast, the shoulders, and the arms; sleeves loose, to allow a free play of the arms, with narrow waistband buttoning with one button; overalls to fasten at the neck behind with two buttons, and at the waist behind with buckle and tongue.

1601. *Belts of all Enlisted Men*—black leather.

1602. *Cartridge-box*—according to pattern in the Ordnance Department.

1603. *Drum-sling*—white webbing; to be provided with a brass drum-stick carriage, according to pattern.

1604. *Knapsack*—of painted canvas, according to pattern now issued by the Quartermaster's Department; the great-coat, when carried, to be neatly folded, not rolled, and covered by the outer flap of the knapsack.

1605. *Haversack*—of painted canvas, with an inside sack unpainted, according to the pattern now issued by the Quartermaster's Department.

1606. *Canteen*—of tin, covered with woolen cloth, of the pattern now issued by the Quartermaster's Department.

MISCELLANEOUS.

1656. General Officers, and Colonels having the brevet rank of General Officers, may, on occasions of ceremony, and when not serving with troops, wear the "dress" and "undress" prescribed by existing regulations.

1657. Officers below the grade of Colonel having brevet rank, will wear the epaulettes and shoulder-straps distinctive of their army rank. In all other respects, their uniform and dress will be that of their respective regiments, corps, or departments, and according to their commissions in the same. Officers above the grade of Lieutenant-Colonel by ordinary commission, having brevet rank, may wear the uniform of their respective regiments or corps, or that of General Officers, according to their brevet rank.

1658. The uniform and dress of the Signal Officer will be that of a Major of the General Staff.

1659. Officers are permitted to wear a plain dark blue body-coat, with the button designating their respective corps, regiments, or departments, without any other mark or ornament upon it. Such a coat, however, is not to be considered as a dress for any military purpose.

1660. In like manner, officers are permitted to wear a buff, white, or blue vest, with the small button of their corps, regiment, or department.

1661. Officers serving with mounted troops are allowed to wear, for stable duty, a plain dark blue cloth jacket, with one or two rows of buttons down the front, according to rank; stand-up collar, sloped in front as that of the uniform coat; shoulder-straps according to rank, but no other ornament.

1662. The hair to be short; the beard to be worn at the pleasure of the individual; but, when worn, to be kept short and neatly trimmed.

1663. *A Band* will wear the uniform of the regiment or corps to which it belongs. The commanding officer may, at the expense of the corps, sanctioned by the Council of Administration, make such *additions* in ornaments as he may judge proper.

ARTICLE LII.

VOLUNTEERS AND MILITIA IN THE SERVICE OF THE UNITED STATES.

1664. Whenever volunteer or drafted militia are called into the service of the United States, by any officer authorized to make such call, the requisition must be made on the Governor of the State or Territory in which the militia are to be raised, and the number of officers, non-commissioned officers, and privates will be stated in the requisition, according to the organization prescribed by the law of the United States.

1665. Before militia are received in the service of the United States, they shall be mustered by an Inspector-General, or some other officer of the regular army, specially designated to muster them.

1666. When volunteers are to be mustered into the service of the United States, they will, at the same time, be minutely examined by the surgeon and assistant surgeon of the regiment, to ascertain whether they have the physical qualifications necessary for the military service. And in case any individual shall be discharged within three months after entering the service, for a disability which existed at that time, he shall receive neither pay nor allowances except subsistence and transportation to his home. The certificate given by the surgeon will, in all cases, state whether the disability existed prior to the date of muster, or was contracted after it.

1667. It shall be the duty of the officer designated to muster and inspect militia, to forward muster-rolls of each company, and of the field and staff of each regiment, *direct* to the Adjutant-General of the Army, Washington; and he will also immediately forward a consolidated return, by regiments and corps, of the force received into service, for the information of the War Department.

1668. *Mustering in*—Reference will be made to the particular act or acts of Congress under which the militia are called into service. If there be no such act, then to the act May 8, 1792, amended by the acts April 18, 1814, and April 20, 1816. Mustering officers will not muster into service a greater number of officers, or of higher rank, than the law prescribes. No officers of the general staff will be mustered or received into service, except such general officers, with their aides-de-camp, as may be required to complete the organization of brigades or divisions.

1669. *Mustering out*—The rolls for this purpose will be compared with those of the first muster. All persons on the first rolls, and absent at the final muster, must be accounted for—whether dead, captured, discharged, or otherwise absent; and if the mustering officer, in any particular case, shall have cause to doubt the report made to be entered on the rolls, he shall demand the oath of one or more persons to prove the fact to his satisfaction; further, he shall take care that not more persons of the several ranks be mustered out of service than were mustered in, if there be an excess over the requisition or beyond the law, nor recognize additions or substitutes, without full satisfaction that the additions or substitutions were regularly made, and at the time reported on the rolls.

1670. Officers mustering in troops will be careful that men from one company or detachment are not borrowed for the occasion, to swell the ranks of others about to be mustered. No volunteer will be mustered into the service who is unable to speak the English language.

1671. Officers charged with the duty of mustering militia will take care that the muster-rolls contain all the information that may in any way affect their pay; the distance from the places of residence to the place of rendezvous or organization, and the date of arrival, must be stated in each case; the date and place of discharge, and the distance thence to the place of residence; all stoppages for articles furnished by the Government must be noted on the rolls; and in cases of absence at the time of discharge of the company, the cause of absence must be stated. When the necessary information cannot be obtained, the mustering officer will state the reason.

1672. If, as has sometimes happened, militia, at the end of a term of service, shall, from the want of a mustering officer, disperse or return home without being regularly mustered out; and if, with a view to a payment, a muster shall afterward be ordered by competent authority, the officer sent for the purpose shall carefully verify all the facts affecting pay, by the oath of one or more of the officers belonging to such militia, in order that full justice may be done.

1673. In all cases of *muster* for *payment*, whether final or otherwise, the mustering officer will give his particular attention to the state and condition of the public property: such as quarters, camp-equipage, means of transportation, arms, accoutrements, ammunition, &c., which have been in the use or possession of the militia to be paid; and if any such public property shall appear to be damaged, or lost, beyond ordinary wear or unavoidable accident, such loss or damage shall be noted on the muster-rolls, in order that the injury or loss sustained by the United States may be stopped from the pay that would otherwise be due to the individual or detachment mustered for payment. *See regulations of the Ordnance Department.* This provision shall be read to all detachments of militia on being mustered into service, and as much oftener as may be deemed necessary.

1674. Payments will, in all cases, be made by the paymasters of the regular army.

1675. Officers of the volunteer service tendering their resignations, will forward them through the intermediate commanders to the officer commanding the department or *corps d'armée* in which they may be serving, who is authorized to grant them honorable discharges. This commander will immediately report his action to the Adjutant-General of the Army, who will communicate the same to the Governor of the State to which the officer belongs. A clear statement of the cause will accompany every resignation.

1676. Vacancies occurring among the commissioned officers in volunteer regiments will be filled by the Governors of the respective States by which the regiments were furnished. Information of such appointments will, in all cases, be furnished to the Adjutant-General of the Army.

APPENDIX.

CHANGES AND ADDITIONS TO ARMY REGULATIONS, UP TO JUNE 25, 1863 [EXTRACTS]

GENERAL REGULATIONS.

1. All correspondence and communication, verbally or by writing, printing, or telegraphing, respecting operations of the army or military movements on land or water, or respecting the troops, camps, arsenals, intrenchments, or military affairs, within the several military districts, by which intelligence shall be, directly or indirectly, given to the enemy, without the authority and sanction of the General in command, be and the same are absolutely prohibited, and persons violating this Regulation will be proceeded against under the 57th Article of War.

5. The insane of the military service are entitled to treatment in the Government Hospital established in Washington. To protect, however, their own interests, as well as those of the Government, it is prescribed by the Secretary of War; that to procure admission into the Hospital, application must be made to the Adjutant General, setting forth the name, rank, company, and regiment of the patient, with a certificate from the surgeon of the regiment as to the duration of the insanity, and whether insane before enlistment. It will likewise be accompanied by the descriptive list of the soldier, containing his pay and clothing accounts. The application should precede the arrival of the soldier in Washington by at least one day.

7. To procure the release of a patient, when cured, or for delivery to his friends, application must again be made to the

Adjutant General, who will procure the necessary authorization, and also cause a statement of his accounts to be made and delivered to him.

8. Guidons and camp colors for the army will be made like the United States flag, with stars and stripes.

9. Paragraph 211, Revised General Regulations, is modified to read as follows: Every military post may have one Sutler, to be appointed by the Secretary of War on the recommendation of the Council of Administration, approved by the Commanding Officer.

11. There shall be inscribed upon the colors or guidons of all regiments and batteries in the service of the United States the names of the battles in which they have borne a meritorious part. These names will also be placed on the Army Register at the head of the list of the officers of each regiment.

13. All property captured by the Army, or seized by any Provost Marshal, or taken up estray, or taken from soldiers marching in the enemy's country, will be turned over to the Chiefs of the Staff Departments to which such property would appertain, on duty with the troops, and will be accounted for by them as captured property, and used for the public service, unless claimed by owners and ordered by the commanding officer to be returned. In such case, the receipts of the owners to whom the property is delivered will be taken therefor. Provost Marshals will make returns to the Adjutant General of all such property and of the disposition made of it, accounting on separate returns for ordnance, quartermaster, subsistence, medical stores, &c., furnishing and procuring the usual invoices and receipts, and charging the officers to whom the property has been delivered, with the same, on the returns.

14. In time of war leaves of absence will only be granted by the Secretary of War, except when the certificate of a medical officer shall show, beyond doubt, that a change of location "is necessary to save life, or prevent *permanent* disability."—(*Paragraph* 186, *General Regulations.*) In such case the Commander of an Army, a Department, or District, may grant not exceeding twenty

days. At the expiration of that time, *if the officer be not able to travel*, he must send a report to the Adjutant General of the Army, accompanied by the certificate of a medical officer of the army, in the usual form, and that he is not able to travel. If it be not practicable to procure such a certificate, in consequence of there being no army physician in the place where the officer resides, the certificate of a citizen physician, *attested by a civil magistrate*, may be substituted.

17. Officers detached from their regiments for Signal duty will report immediately for orders to the Signal Officer of the Army; after which they will not be relieved from such duty, except by orders from the Adjutant General of the Army.

19. When an officer returns to his command after having overstaid his leave of absence, he may be tried by a court-martial for this as a military offence, or a commission may be appointed by the commanding officer of his division, army corps, or army, as the case may be, to investigate his case, and to determine whether or not he was absent from proper cause; and if there should be found to be such proper cause, he will be entitled to pay during such absence. The proceedings of such commission will be sent to the Adjutant General of the Army for the approval of the Secretary of War. Such commissions will consist of not less than three nor over five commissioned officers.

21. The laws of the United States and the general laws of war authorize, in certain cases, the seizure and conversion of private property for the subsistence, transportation, and other uses of the army; but this must be distinguished from pillage; and the taking of property for *public* purposes is very different from its conversion to *private* uses. All property lawfully taken from the enemy, or from the inhabitants of an enemy's country, instantly becomes *public* property, and must be used and accounted for as such. The 52d Article of War authorizes the penalty of death for pillage or plundering, and other articles authorize severe punishments for any officer or soldier who shall sell, embezzle, misapply, or waste military stores, or who shall permit the waste or

misapplication of any such public property. The penalty is the same whether the offence be committed in our own or in an enemy's territory.

22. All property, public or private, taken from alleged enemies, must be inventoried and duly accounted for. If the property taken be claimed as private, receipts must be given to such claimants or their agents. Officers will be held strictly responsible for all property taken by them or by their authority, and it must be accounted for, the same as any other public property.

23. Where foraging parties are sent out for provisions or other stores, the commanding officer of such party will be held accountable for the conduct of his command, and will make a true report of all property taken.

24. No officer or soldier will, without authority, leave his colors or ranks, to take private property, or to enter a private house for that purpose. All such acts are punishable with death, and an officer who permits them is equally as guilty as the actual pillager.

27. Officers of the Army and of Volunteers detailed for duty in the Engineers or other branches of the staff, are not, as a matter of course, entitled to the pay, emoluments, and allowances of cavalry officers. But, when ordered by the proper authority to be mounted, and when so mounted at their own expense, they are entitled to such pay, emoluments, and allowances.

28. No officer will hereafter be relieved from his command and sent to report in Washington without the authority of the War Department. Where subordinate officers are guilty of military offences, or are negligent, or incompetent, it is the duty of the Commander to have them tried for their offences, or examined in regard to their incompetency, by a proper court or commission; and this duty cannot be evaded by sending them to Washington.

31. Paragraph 1416, Army Regulations, is so amended as to authorize issues, without payment, of equipments and arms necessary to the performance of such duty to officers detailed for special duty requiring them to be mounted; and for which service

they receive no additional compensation. Officers shall receipt and account for all equipments or arms so issued to them.

32. All quartermasters and commissaries will personally attend to the reception and issue of supplies for their commands, and will keep themselves informed of the condition of the depots, roads, and other communications.

38. The only members of their Staff whom General Officers are authorized to take with them, when detached from, or otherwise leaving their commands, are their ordinary Aides-de-Camp— those selected in accordance with the acts of July 22 and 29, 1861, sections 3 and 4, respectively, and of July 17, 1862, section 10.

ARMY TRAINS AND BAGGAGE.

41. There will be allowed for headquarters train of an Army Corps, *four* wagons; of a Division or Brigade, *three*; a full Infantry Regiment, *six*; and a Light Artillery Battery or Squadron of Cavalry, *three*. In no case will this allowance be exceeded, but always proportionably reduced according to the number of officers and men actually present. All surplus wagons will be turned over to the Chief Quartermaster to be organized, under direction of the Commanding Generals, into supply trains, or sent to the nearest depot. The requisite supply trains, their size depending upon the state of the roads and character of the campaign, will be organized by the Chief Quartermaster, with the approval of the Commanding Generals, subject to the control of the War Department.

42. The wagons allowed to a regiment, battery, or squadron, must carry nothing but forage for the teams, cooking utensils, and rations for the troops, hospital stores, and officers' baggage. One wagon to each regiment will transport exclusively hospital supplies, under the direction of the Regimental Surgeon; the one for regimental headquarters will carry the grain for the officers' horses; and the three allowed for each battery or squadron will be at least half loaded with grain for their own teams. Stores in bulk

and ammunition will be carried in the regular or special supply trains.

QUARTERMASTER'S DEPARTMENT.

48. Paragraph 156 is amended so that in addition to the reward of five dollars for the apprehension and delivery of a deserter to an officer of the army at the nearest military post or depot, the transportation and reasonable expenses of the duty will be paid in the case of each deserter arrested and delivered since the 31st day of July, 1862.

49. For the purpose of preserving accurate and permanent records of deceased soldiers, and their place of burial, the Quartermaster General of the United States Army shall cause to be printed, and to be placed in every General and Post Hospital of the Army, blank books and forms corresponding with the accompanying duplicate forms, for preserving said records. The Quartermaster will also provide proper means for a registered head-board, to be secured at the head of each soldier's grave, as follows: Whenever any soldier or officer of the United States Army dies, it shall be the duty of the commanding officer of the military corps or department in which such person dies, to cause the regulation and forms provided in the foregoing directions to the Quartermaster General to be properly executed. Any Adjutant, or Acting Adjutant (or commander) of a military post or company, immediately upon the reception of a copy of any mortuary record from a military company, shall transmit the same to the Adjutant General at Washington.

50. Transportation by express agency being liable to abuse, and very expensive, is prohibited by the Secretary of War, on public account, except in cases of great emergency, for which the officer ordering or sending the stores shall be responsible.

51. Paragraph 1068.—Military storekeepers are entitled to the same allowance of fuel as first lieutenants of the army.

52. Medical cadets and hospital stewards will be entitled each to one room as quarters, and fuel therefor.

53. Paragraph 1121, of the Revised Regulations for the Army, of 1861, is amended by adding as follows: In special cases of hard service or exposure, the Quartermaster General may authorize the ration of grain to be increased not more than three pounds, upon a report recommending it by the Chief Quartermaster serving in a Military Department, or with an Army in the field.

64. The assistant commissary generals of subsistence, assistant surgeons general, medical inspectors general, and medical inspectors are entitled to the same number of rooms as offices, and fuel and furniture therefor, as are allowed to officers of the Quartermaster's Department who have the same rank.

67. Paragraph 1156 is modified to read as follows:

Water-proof ponchoes will be issued to mounted troops as articles of clothing, and charged to them in their respective clothing accounts. Water-proof blankets will, in like manner, be issued to foot troops, and charged to the soldiers who receive them.

68. Paragraph 1158 is modified to read as follows:

Officers receiving clothing, or camp and garrison equipage, will render monthly returns of it to the Quartermaster General.

MEDICAL DEPARTMENT.

69. Surgeons from civil life who tender their services for the sick and wounded in the field, under the invitation of the Secretary of War, will each be allowed, while so employed, the use of a public horse, a tent, the necessary servants, and the privilege of purchasing stores from the Subsistence Department.

71. Paragraph 1305 Army Regulations is hereby so modified that private physicians, employed as medical officers with an army in the field in time of war, may be allowed a sum not to exceed one hundred and twenty-five dollars per month, besides transportation in kind.

72. The exercise of the powers given the Medical Inspectors of the Army to discharge soldiers for disability, is suspended until their duties in this respect are defined by Regulations to be published hereafter.

80. The general hospitals are under the direction of the Surgeon General. When it is expedient and advisable, sick and wounded soldiers may, under the direction of the Surgeon General, be transferred in parties, but not in individual cases, to other hospitals.

PAY DEPARTMENT.

82. The Paymaster General is authorized to change the stations of Paymasters within the limits of the pay districts which have been or may be arranged by him, whenever he may deem it necessary for the interests of the service.

ORDNANCE DEPARTMENT.

83. Paragraph 905, General Regulations, is amended by inserting after the word "Companies," in the third line, the following: "and armorers for repairing arms of regiments serving as Infantry or Cavalry."

84. The fourth line of paragraph 1023, General Regulations, is modified to read as follows: "may require—the *sale* of ordnance and ordnance stores excepted," &c.

85. All Captains of Companies are hereby required to report quarterly to the Chief of Ordnance the kind of arms in use by their companies, their opinion of the suitableness of the arm, the general extent of service, and the number requiring repairs since the previous report. (Additional instructions are published by the Ordnance Department, and may be obtained by officers interested by application to the chief of ordnance.)

RECRUITING SERVICE.

86. Paragraphs 924, 931, 933, 934, 1211, and 1212, Revised Regulations for the Army, of 1861, are modified to read as follows:

87. Tours of inspection by superintendents will be made only on instructions from the Adjutant General's Office; but superintendents may order officers to visit branch or auxiliary

rendezvous under their charge, not oftener than once a week. The branch rendezvous to be established only by orders from superintendents, and not to be more than fifteen miles distant from the main rendezvous.

88. No person under the age of eighteen years is to be enlisted or re-enlisted without the written consent of his parent, guardian, or master. Recruiting officers must be very particular in ascertaining the true age of the recruit.

89. If the recruit be a minor under eighteen years of age, his parent, guardian, or master must sign a consent to his enlisting, which will be added to the preceding declaration in the following form, &c.

90. The forms of declaration, and of consent, in case of a minor under eighteen, having been signed and witnessed, the recruit will then be duly examined, &c.

91. Issues of provisions will be made on the usual ration returns, and board will be furnished on a return showing the number of the party, the days, and dates. A ration in kind may be allowed to one laundress at each principal rendezvous.

94. The recruiting service in the various States for the volunteer forces already in service, and for those that may be received, is placed under charge of general superintendents for those States, respectively, with general depots for the collection and instruction of recruits.

95. Both the superintendents and the location of the depots are announced in orders from the Adjutant General's Office.

98. Commanding officers of volunteer regiments, or independent companies, will take measures to keep the strength of their commands up to the maximum standard of organization.

99. For this purpose two commissioned officers, with one non-commissioned officer or private from each company, will be detailed, from time to time, to report in person to the superintendents of the recruiting service for their respective States. The full number will not be detailed if a less number will suffice to fill up the regiment.

104. Mustering officers will muster into service and administer the oath of allegiance to such regiments or recruits brought to them as may present conclusive evidence of their acceptance by the War Department.

109. Superintendents will keep their depots supplied with sufficient clothing for issues to recruits, and with the arms necessary for their instruction.

111. To facilitate the raising of volunteer regiments, officers recruiting therefor are authorized to muster their men into service as enrolled. As soon as mustered, these men will be sent, with descriptive lists, to the camps of rendezvous, at which places the oath of allegiance will be duly administered by a civil magistrate, or an officer of the regular army, preferably by the latter. The cost of transportation from place of muster-in to camps of rendezvous will be paid by the quartermaster at the latter station.

PRISONERS OF WAR.

117. Officers and soldiers of the United States who are or may become prisoners of war shall, during their imprisonment, be entitled to and receive the same pay as if they were doing active duty.

118. The rations of prisoners held in the rebel States shall be commuted for and during the period of their imprisonment; the commutation to be rated at cost price. To entitle a soldier to this commutation he must furnish to the Commissary General of Prisoners such evidence of the fact of capture and time of detention as he may consider necessary, to be laid before the Secretary of War, and if approved, a certificate will be issued by the Commissary General of Prisoners, on which payment will be made by the Subsistence Department.

119. A general commanding in the field, or a department, will make arrangements for the safe-keeping and reasonable comfort of his prisoners. For this purpose he will place them under a guard already on duty, or detach a guard for the special service.

The general will give no order exchanging prisoners, or releasing them, except under instructions from the Secretary of War.

120. In emergencies admitting of no delay the general will act upon his own authority, and give any order in relation to his prisoners the public interest might require, promptly reporting his proceedings to the War Department through the Adjutant General.

121. In time of war a Commissary General of Prisoners will be announced, whose general duties will be those of an inspector, and all communications relating to prisoners will pass through him. Depots for prisoners will be designated by the Secretary of War, to which suitable and permanent guards will be assigned, the whole to be under the orders of the Commissary General of Prisoners. He will establish regulations for issuing clothing to prisoners, and . . . he is authorized to grant paroles to prisoners on the recommendation of the medical officer attending the prison in cases of extreme illness, but under no other circumstances.

125. The Commissary General of Prisoners has charge of the United States officers and men on parole, and correspondence relating to them. All details concerning them will pass through him.

127. The principle being recognized that medical officers and chaplains should not be held as prisoners of war, all medical officers and chaplains so held by the United States will be immediately and unconditionally discharged.

128. Whenever prisoners of war are released on parole and sent through the lines, the officers who release them will immediately send rolls to the Commissary General of Prisoners, containing an exact list of the prisoners' names, rank, regiment, and company, date and place of capture, and date and place of parole. These rolls are indispensable in effecting exchanges of prisoners.

UNIFORM.

130. In time of actual field service, officers of Cavalry, Artillery, and Infantry are permitted to wear the light blue overcoat prescribed for enlisted men of the mounted corps.

131. The uniform for Chaplains of the Army will be plain black frock coat with standing collar, and one row of nine black buttons; plain black pantaloons; black felt hat, or army forage cap, without ornament. On occasions of ceremony, a plain chapeau de bras may be worn.

132. The following change is made in the uniform trowsers of regimental officers and enlisted men: The cloth to be sky-blue mixture. The welt for officers, and stripes for non-commissioned officers of Infantry, to be of dark blue.

133. The following uniform has been adopted for the Invalid Corps:

Jacket—Of sky-blue kersey, with dark-blue trimmings, cut like the jacket for United States cavalry, to come well down on the loins and abdomen.

Trowsers—Present regulation, sky-blue.

Forage Cap—Present regulation.

134. The following uniform has been adopted for officers of the Invalid Corps:

Frock Coat—Of sky-blue cloth, with dark-blue velvet collar and cuffs—in all other respects, according to the present pattern for officers of Infantry.

Shoulder Straps—According to present regulations, but worked on dark-blue velvet.

Pantaloons—Of sky-blue cloth, with double stripe of dark-blue cloth down the outer seam, each stripe one-half inch wide, with space between of three-eighths of an inch.

MUSTERING VOLUNTEERS INTO AND OUT OF THE SERVICE OF THE UNITED STATES.

135. The regulations governing this branch of service are published in pamphlet form, and distributed to the Army by the Adjutant General.

DRAFTING.

136. The regulations governing this branch of service are published in pamphlet form, and distributed to those officers who may require them in the performance of their duties by the Provost Marshal General.

Table of Pay, Subsistence, etc.

TABLE OF PAY, SUBSISTENCE, ETC. ALLOWED BY LAW TO THE OFFICERS OF THE ARMY.

RANK AND CLASSIFICATION OF OFFICERS	PAY. Per Month.	SUBSISTENCE. Number of Rations per day.	SUBSISTENCE. Monthly Commutation Value.	SERVANTS. Number of Servants allowed.	SERVANTS. Monthly Commutation Value.	Total Monthly Pay.	FORAGE FURNISHED FOR HORSES. In time of War.	FORAGE FURNISHED FOR HORSES. In time of Peace.
General Officers.	$ c.		$ c.		$ c.	$ c.	& for forage	$50
Lieutenant-General	270 00	40	300 00	4	90 00	720 00		2
Aides-de-camp and Military Secretary to } Lieutenant-General, each	80 00	5	45 00	2	45 00	170 00		5
Major-General	220 00	15	135 00	4	90 00	445 00		2
Senior Aide-de-camp to General-in-Chief	80 00	4	36 00	2	47 00	163 00		2
Aide-de-camp, in addition to pay, &c. of } Lieutenant or Captain	24 00					24 00		4
Brigadier-General	124 00	12	108 00	3	67 50	299 50		2
Aide-de-camp, in addition to pay, &c. of } Lieutenant	20 00					11*		
Adjutant-General's Department.								
Adjutant-General—Brigadier-General	124 00	24	216 00	3	67 00	407 50		4
Assistant Adjutant-General—Colonel	110 00	6	54 00	2	47 00	211 00		2
Assistant Adjutant-General—Lieut.-Col	95 00	5	45 00	2	47 00	187 00		2
Assistant Adjutant-General—Major	80 00	4	36 00	2	47 00	163 00		2
Judge-Advocate-General—Colonel	110 00	6	54 00	2	47 00	211 00		2
Judge-Advocate—Major	80 00	4	36 00	2	47 00	163 00		2
" (Division)—Major	80 00	4	36 00	2	47 00	163 00		2

Inspector-General's Department.							
Inspector-General—Colonel	110 00	6	54 00	2	47 00	211 00	2
Assistant Inspector-General—Major	80 00	4	36 00	2	47 00	163 00	2
Signal Department.							
Signal Officer—Colonel	110 00	6	54 00	2	47 00	211 00	2
Quartermaster's Department.							
Quartermaster-General—Brig.-Gen	124 00	24	216 00	3	67 00	407 00	4
Assistant Quartermaster-General—Col	110 00	6	54 00	2	47 00	211 00	2
Deputy Quartermaster-General—Lt.-Col	95 00	5	45 00	2	47 00	187 00	2
Quartermaster—Major	80 00	4	36 00	2	47 00	163 00	2
Assistant Quartermaster—Captain	70 00	4	36 00	1	23 50	129 50	2
Subsistence Department.							
Commissary-General of Subs.—Brig.-Gen	124 00	12	108 00	3	67 00	299 00	4
Assistant Commissary-General of Subsistence—Lieutenant-Colonel	95 00	5	45 00	2	47 00	187 00	2
Commissary of Subsistence—Major	80 00	4	36 00	2	47 00	163 00	2
Commissary of Subsistence—Captain	70 00	4	36 00	1	23 50	129 50	2
Assistant Commissary of Subsistence, in addition to pay, &c. of Lieutenant	20 00	...	...	...	...	11*	...
Medical Department.							
Surgeon-General—Brigadier-General	124 00	12	108 00	3	67 00	299 50	4
Assistant Surgeon-General	110 00	6	54 00	2	47 00	211 00	2
Medical Inspector-General	110 00	6	54 00	2	47 00	211 00	2
Medical Inspectors	95 00	5	45 00	2	47 00	187 00	2
Surgeons of ten years' service	80 00	8	72 00	2	47 00	199 00	2
Surgeons of less than ten years' service	80 00	4	36 00	2	47 00	163 00	2
Assistant Surgeons of ten years' service	70 00	8	72 00	1	23 50	165 50	2
Assistant Surgeons of five years' service	70 00	4	36 00	1	23 50	129 50	2
Assistant Surgeons of less than five years' service	53 33	4	36 00	1*	23 50	112 83	2
Pay Department.							
Paymaster-General, $2740 per annum						288 33	
Deputy Paymaster-General	96 00	5	43 00	2	47 00	187 00	2
Paymaster	80 00	4	36 00	2	47 00	163 00	2

Table of Pay, Subsistence, etc.

TABLE OF PAY, SUBSISTENCE, FORAGE.—Continued.

RANK AND CLASSIFICATION OF OFFICERS.	PAY. Per Month.	SUBSISTENCE. Number of Rations per day.	SUBSISTENCE. Monthly Commutation Value.	SERVANTS. Number of Servants allowed.	SERVANTS. Monthly Commutation Value.	Total Monthly Pay.	FORAGE FURNISHED FOR HORSES. In time of War.	FORAGE FURNISHED FOR HORSES. In time of Peace.
Officers of the Corps of Engineers, Corps of Topographical Engineers, and Ordnance Department.								
Chief of Ordnance—Brigadier-Genera...	124 00	24	216 00	3	67 50	407 50		4
Colonel	110 00	6	54 00	2	47 00	211 00		2
Lieutenant-Colonel	95 00	5	45 00	2	47 00	187 00		2
Major	80 00	4	36 00	2	47 00	163 00		2
Captain	70 00	4	36 00	2	23 50	129 50		2
First Lieutenant	53 33	4	36 00	1	23 50	112 83		2
Second Lieutenant	53 33	4	36 00	1	23 50	112 83		2
Brevet Second Lieutenant	53 33	4	36 00	1	23 50	112 83		2
Officers of Mounted Dragoons, Cavalry, Riflemen, and Light Artillery.								
Colonel	110 00	6	54 00	2	47 00	211 00		2
Lieutenant-Colonel	95 00	5	45 00	2	47 00	187 00		2
Major	80 00	4	36 00	2	47 00	163 00		2
Captain	70 00	4	36 00	2	23 50	129 50		2
First Lieutenant	53 33	4	36 00	1	23 50	112 83		2
Second Lieutenant	53 33	4	36 00	1	23 50	112 83		2
Brevet Second Lieutenant	53 33	4	36 00	1	23 50	112 83		2
Adjutant
Reg'l Quartermaster { in addition to pay of Lieutenant.
Reg'l Commissary	10 00					10 00		

Officers of Artillery and Infantry.

Colonel	95 00	6	54 00	2	45 00 194 00	2
Lieutenant-Colonel	80 00	5	45 00	2	45 00 170 00	2
Major	70 00	4	36 00	2	45 00 161 00	2
Captain	60 00	4	36 00	1	22 50 118 50	……
First Lieutenant	50 00	4	36 00	1	22 50 108 50	……
Second Lieutenant	45 00	4	36 00	1	22 50 103 50	……
Brevet Second Lieutenant	45 00	4	36 00	1	22 50 103 50	……
Adjutant, in addition to pay, &c. of Lieut.	10 00	……	……	……	…… 10 00	2
Reg'l Quartermaster, in addition to pay, &c. of Lieutenant	10 00	……	……	……	…… 10 00	2

Military Storekeepers.

Attached to the Quartermaster's Department; at armories, and at arsenals of construction; the storekeeper at Watertown Arsenal, and storekeepers of ordnance serving in Oregon, California, and New Mexico, $1490 per annum.	……	……	……	……	……	……
At all other arsenals, $1040 per annum	100 00	2	18 00	……	…… 118 00	……
Chaplains	……	……	……	……	……	1

Paymaster's clerks, $700 per annum, and one ration (75 cents) per day when on duty.

The officer in command of a company is allowed $10 per month for the responsibility of clothing, arms, and accoutrements.—Act 2 March, 1827, Sec. 2.

* Subaltern officers, employed on the *General Staff*, and receiving increased pay therefor. are not entitled to the additional or fourth ration provided by the Act of 2 March, 1827, Sec. 2.

Every commissioned officer below the rank of Brigadier-General receives one additional ration per day for every five years' service.—Act 5 July, 1836, Sec. 12, and 7 July, 1838, Sec. 9.

Forage is commuted only when the Government cannot furnish it in kind, and then at $8 per month for each horse actually kept by the officer.

2 U

Table of Pay.

MONTHLY PAY OF NON-COMMISSIONED OFFICERS, PRIVATES, ETC.

CAVALRY.

Sergeant-Major	$21 00	Hospital Steward	$30 00
Quartermaster-Sergeant	21 00	Corporal	14 00
Chief Bugler or Trumpeter	21 00	Bugler or Trumpeter	13 00
First Sergeant	20 00	Farrier and Blacksmith	15 00
Sergeant	17 00	Private	13 00
Saddler Sergeant	21 00	Veterinary Surgeon	75 00
Commissary Sergeant	21 00	African Under Cooks	10 00

ORDNANCE.

Sergeant	$34 00	Saddler	$14 00
Corporal	20 00	Private, first class	17 00
Wagoner	14 00	Private, second class	13 00

ARTILLERY AND INFANTRY.

Sergeant-Major	$21 00	Corporal	$13 00
Quartermaster-Sergeant	21 00	Artificer, artillery	15 00
Commissary Sergeant	21 00	Private	13 00
First Sergeant	20 00	Principal Musician	21 00
Sergeant	17 00	Musician	12 00
Hospital Stewards	30 00	African Under Cooks	10 00

SAPPERS, MINERS, AND PONTONIERS.

Sergeant	$34 00	Private, second class	$13 00
Corporal	20 00	Musician	12 00
Private, first class	17 00	African Under Cooks	10 00

BRIGADE BANDS.

Leader	$45 00	Eight of the Band	$17 00
Four of the Band	34 00	Four of the Band	20 00

Medical Cadets	$30 00	Matron	$6 00
Hospital Steward, first class	22 00	Female Nurses, 40 cents per day and one ration.	
" " second class	20 00		

Two dollars per month is to be retained from the pay of each private soldier until the expiration of his term of enlistment, and 12½ cents per month from all enlisted men, for the support of the "Soldier's Home."

All enlisted men are entitled to $2 per month additional pay for re-enlisting, and $1 per month for each subsequent period of five years' service, provided they re-enlist within one month after the expiration of their term.

Volunteers and militia, when called into service of the United States, are entitled to the same pay, allowances, &c., as regulars.

Medical Storekeepers, same as Military Storekeepers, Quartermaster's Department.

The Stackpole
Military Classics Series

Authentic hardcover reproductions and reprints of key Civil War military manuals and reference books-especially useful for students, writers, historians, reenactors, and those interested in military operations during the American Civil War (1861–1865).

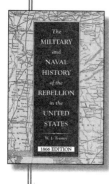

THE MILITARY AND NAVAL HISTORY OF THE REBELLION IN THE UNITED STATES
1866 EDITION
William Jewett Tenney

The first comprehensive history of the American Civil War (1861–1865), it contains accounts of all military and naval campaigns, battles, and major skirmishes copiously illustrated with maps and diagrams and packed with original documents, reports, and correspondence.

$39.95, HC, 880 pages, 50 illustrations, 10 steel engravings, 6¹/₈ x 9¹/₄ (original format)

"One of the outstanding events of 19th century publishing . . . a meticulously crafted volume."
—MILITARY HISTORY

"This huge work has withstood the test of many years as a major work of the history of the Civil War."
—THE CIVIL WAR COURIER

1-800-732-3669 • *www.stackpolebooks.com*

The Stackpole
Military Classics Series

THE 1865
CUSTOMS OF SERVICE
FOR OFFICERS OF THE ARMY
A HANDBOOK OF THE DUTIES
OF EACH GRADE LIEUTENANT
TO LIEUT. GENERAL

August V. Kautz

Reproduction edition of the authentic "how-to"
guide to commissioned officer duties, military
leadership responsibilities, and command practices. Includes all branches of the Army.

*$15.95, HC, 384 pages, 7 diagrams,
2 maps, 8 forms, 3$^{1}/_{2}$ x 5 (original format)*

1-800-732-3669 • *www.stackpolebooks.com*

The Stackpole
Military Classics Series

THE 1865 CUSTOMS OF SERVICE FOR NON-COMMISSIONED OFFICERS AND SOLDIERS
A HANDBOOK FOR THE RANK AND FILE OF THE ARMY
August V. Kautz

An 1865 soldier's handbook of the duties and functions of each enlisted rank in the Army (private to sergeant major) and each branch of service (Infantry, Artillery, Cavalry, Quartermaster, Signal, Medical, etc.) and how they are performed. A fascinating description military service in America's Civil War armies.

$14.95, HC, 304 pages, 5 illustrations, 3¹/₂ x 5 (original format)

1-800-732-3669 • *www.stackpolebooks.com*

The Stackpole
Military Classics Series

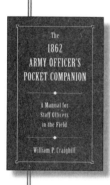

THE 1862 ARMY OFFICER'S POCKET COMPANION
A MANUAL FOR STAFF OFFICERS IN THE FIELD
William P. Craighill

Unique summary of military science as it stood at the beginning of the Civil War. Excellent description of strategies, tactics, and operations of all components of the Army. Written by a West Point faculty member at the direction of the War Department.

$19.95, HC, 320 pages, 26 illustrations, 3⅝ x 5⅞ (original format)

1-800-732-3669 • *www.stackpolebooks.com*

The Stackpole
Military Classics Series

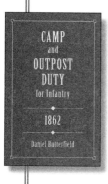

CAMP AND OUTPOST DUTY FOR INFANTRY

1862

Daniel Butterfield

Standing orders, extracts from the Revised Regulations for the Army dealing with camp and outpost duty, plus rules of health, maxims for soldiers, and duties of officers.

$11.95, HC, 128 pages, 4 illustrations, 3¹/₂ x 5 (original format)

1-800-732-3669 • *www.stackpolebooks.com*

The Stackpole
Military Classics Series

THE 1863 U.S.
INFANTRY TACTICS
INFANTRY OF THE LINE,
LIGHT INFANTRY, AND RIFLEMEN

2ND EDITION

U.S. War Department

Official guide for the training and employment
of the infantry from individual soldier to
regimental level. Instructions for skirmishers,
dictionary of military terms, and sheet music
for all 48 Army bugle calls.

*$21.95, HC, 592 pages, 76 illustrations,
3¹/₂ x 5 (original format)*

1-800-732-3669 • *www.stackpolebooks.com*

The Stackpole
Military Classics Series

THE 1862 U.S.
CAVALRY TACTICS
INSTRUCTIONS, FORMATIONS,
MANŒUVERS
Philip St. Geo. Cooke

Written at War Department direction for the
training and employment of cavalry in battle.
Over 200 maneuvers; manuals of arms for sword,
pistol, and rifle. All voice and bugle commands,
including music for all 38 cavalry bugle calls.
Definitions of cavalry terms.

$19.95, HC, 416 pages, 82 illustrations,
3¹/₂ x 5⁷/₈ (original format)

1-800-732-3669 • *www.stackpolebooks.com*